Manitoba, Naturally
Scenic Secrets of Manitoba

First Edition

Bill Stilwell

Manitoba, Naturally

**Published by
William Street Publishing**

**P.O. Box 1427, Neepawa, MB
R0J 1H0 • Canada
(204) 476-5210
manitobanaturally@mts.net**

Printed in Canada
First Edition
ISBN 0-9781001-0-7 (softcover)
ISBN 0-9781001-1-5 (hardcover)

Author	Bill Stilwell
Book Design	Innovative Media Group
Maps	Alex Martin
Editing assistance	Herb Goulden
	Georgette Hutlet
	Mandy Moran
Photography	Bill Stilwell and guests*
	*other photographers are credited where photos appear

Acknowledgements:

I would like to express appreciation and thanks to many people and groups who helped with the development of this book including: Mary Birt, Christie Borkowsky, Pete Borowski, Dan Chranowski, David Clayton, Cal Cuthbert, Ken DeSmet, Jack Dubois, Jim Duncan, Gene Fortney, Cary Hamel, Harry Harris, Daryll Hedman, Kelly Leavesley, Mike Moore, John Morgan, Tom Moran, Valerie Pankratz, Leigh Patterson, Glenn Peterson, Gerry Reichseidler, Laura Reeves, Ian Ripley, Dave Roberts, Ken Ulrich, Dr. Al Rogosin, Ken Schykulski, Dan Soprovich, Tim Sopuck, Andrew Stilwell, Dr. Richard Westwood, John Whitaker, Reto Zach, E. Stilwell, Sustainable Development Innovations Fund, Ducks Unlimited, Nature Conservancy Canada, Riding Mountain Biosphere Reserve.

— Bill Stilwell

Manitoba, Naturally
Scenic Secrets of Manitoba

cedar waxwing, Brent Jones

Manitoba is rich in scenic beauty. Our parks, rivers, lakes and natural spaces provide a dramatic landscape of distinctive landforms that are nothing short of spectacular with abundant wild animals, birds and native plants. This is Manitoba at its best; and, *Manitoba, Naturally.*

Manitoba is all about diversity and natural splendour. Canadian Shield, boreal forest, luxuriant river valleys, arctic tundra and the prairie potholes; there are far too many features to list. As well, Manitoba's diverse landscape is also responsible for our abundant plants and animals.

It is a daunting challenge to find every scenic location, let alone explore them all. Some of the best places have been well kept secrets that may only be known locally.

If you have friends or relatives living near one of these scenic locations, chances are they may take you for a visit. If not, let this book guide you to experience Manitoba's natural beauty with that same familiarity of an old friend showing you around.

Regardless of your knowledge, skill level or sense of adventure, you will find new outdoor adventures with the help of this book. Some of the locations will provide interesting or unique scenery and spectacular views, while others offer the sights and sounds of nature and wildlife.

Contents

About the book

Manitoba, Naturally is divided into eleven chapters, each containing four to eight sites, and when clustered together, they form circle tours.

As well, the book systematically covers all major ecological zones in the province — those areas that exhibit similar characteristics of landforms and climate and habitats. If you visited them all, you would sample nearly every ecosystem in Manitoba. An ecosystem is a complex or community of organisms that interact in their environment as a unit. By visiting these diverse natural regions, you could see a broad range of birds, animals and plants that depend on each different type of habitat.

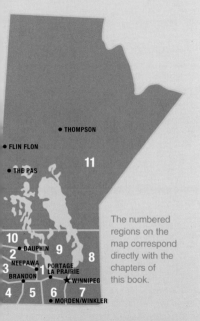

THOMPSON

FLIN FLON

THE PAS

11

10

DAUPHIN 9

NEEPAWA

BRANDON 8

PORTAGE LA PRAIRIE

WINNIPEG

2

3

4 5 6 7

MORDEN/WINKLER

The numbered regions on the map correspond directly with the chapters of this book.

At the beginning of each chapter is a photograph of one of the region's major attractions: plant or animals or an easily recognizable scenic view.

These photographs represent major attractions that are not specifically described in the book.

These locations offer a combination of unique scenery and superb wildlife viewing opportunities. In many cases the directions provided will get you into the right area, but you must travel around, or leave your vehicle and explore to gain the most from your experience.

And remember, depending on the time of year and even the time of day, the animals and plants you hope to see are not always easy to find. For example, birds that migrate may not be present during midsummer, and many wild species are most active during early mornings and late evenings. As well, wildflowers bloom for only a short period and the timing varies with the weather conditions.

Keep as quiet as possible, for most wildlife usually hear you before you see them. Be patient. Although not visible, birds and other wildlife may be nearby, so listen for their calls or songs. It is amazing how the woods and grasslands come alive when you are concealed, and quiet.

A good pair of binoculars or a spotting scope helps to get a better view without having to move closer to birds and animals. Sometimes it is simply best to stay in the vehicle when wildlife is nearby. Many creatures are easily frightened, so keeping your distance provides the least disturbance. Remember to take a camera to record your visit.

Always exercise caution; don't travel down back roads after rains or snow. Many back roads are not maintained year-round, so consult with local municipal offices or the local park or conservation offices before venturing out.

Always wear good footwear, take rain gear, maps, a compass, food, water, matches and insect repellent. Be sure to let someone know where you will be travelling and when you are expected back. You will be well prepared if you plan for the conditions and any potential problems that may arise.

This book is designed to help you enjoy and experience some of the best that Manitoba's outdoors has to offer — but we offer no guarantees. The rest is up to you and remember, this is *Manitoba, Naturally*!

Best time to visit
seasonal icons

 Spring   Summer   Autumn   Winter

Jargon and abbreviations

- **Acres:** Our survey system divides land into square miles. While Canada uses metric, our survey system commonly uses acres not hectares.

- **Kms:** kilometres. One km equals 0.62 miles. Ten kms is about six miles.

- **WMA:** wildlife management area. These are public lands.

- **Crown land:** public land owned by the Province of Manitoba.

- **IBA:** Important Bird Area as designated by Birdlife International.

- **NCC:** Nature Conservancy of Canada.

- **RMBR:** Riding Mountain Biosphere Reserve; designated by the United Nations.

- **Staging area:** locations where birds stop to rest during migration.

Sightings

A list of species that could be found at each site, but with no guarantee.

Directions

Most directions are straightforward but you also need a highway map.

Westlake chapter 1

Park Lake, Neepawa

Lake Irwin — Boggy Creek

purple finch

Sightings

song sparrow
American redstart
red-winged blackbird
warbling vireo
common yellowthroat

From Neepawa, go 1.6 kilometres (km) south on Highway 5. Turn east and go 0.6 km.

Songbirds swiftly dart from branch to branch, using the river bottom and shoreline as cover. A careful observer is sure to notice several, but even the uninitiated will catch their cheerful songs.

Groups of amateur ornithologists often visit Boggy Creek, a spot guaranteed to produce interesting bird observations. An astounding variety of neo-tropical migratory birds is found here. Neo-tropical birds are songbirds that migrate each autumn to warmer climates.

Boggy Creek is fed by the Assiniboine Delta Aquifer, a feature created during the most recent period of glaciation as a delta of glacial Lake Agassiz. The creek starts many kilometres south and is bordered by a healthy riparian zone on either side. When it reaches Lake Irwin, it widens and joins another creek, known as Brookdale Drain. About 1.5 km farther north it joins Stoney Creek to become the Whitemud River.

These riparian areas are extremely productive habitat. Plants and woody shrubs favouring moist sites thrive near the water while drier conditions prevail farther back. Along with shelter, these moist lowlands give way to uplands producing an abundance of fruit and seed-bearing native plants desired by many wildlife species.

Lake Irwin is a small waterbody created by a dam across Boggy Creek. It was initially created to impound water for drinking and irrigation but over time the lake has matured,

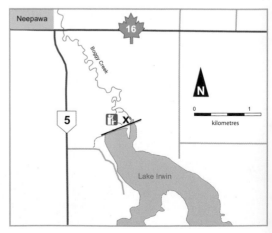

vegetation emerged, and now it also provides valuable habitat for a variety of birds and other wildlife.

Much of the lakeshore is ringed with vegetation forming a web connecting adjacent habitat that encourages wildlife movement. Songbirds, in particular, use these shorelines. Below the dam, a wild tangle of shrubs and trees is alive with songbirds during migration season. This nesting area often attracts organized birdwatchers.

The open water of Lake Irwin affords staging habitat for a variety of waterfowl species. Depending upon migration patterns, it sometimes produces a chance to see large flocks of snow geese. A resident Canada goose population nests here. Migrating loons, grebes and bald eagles also visit for short periods.

This region is an oddity, one of the most unique places in North America because four major natural regions converge near here. The Aspen-oak Parkland, Souris Till Plain (prairies), Western Uplands (boreal forest and transition zone atop the Riding Mountain escarpment) and the Assiniboine Delta (sandhills) all draw together — likely the only place where this occurs. Unique plant life, birds and other wildlife inhabit each of these major landforms.

purple prairie-clover

Roes Lake

snow geese

marsh hedge-nettle

great blue heron

Sightings

black tern
kildeer
Wilson's phalarope
ruffed and sharp-tailed grouse
northern pintail

From Neepawa, go 16 km north on Provincial Highway 5 and then 13 km east on Provincial Road (PR) 265. The wetland is on the south side.

Keep your head down is the best advice when visiting Roes Lake, or Rowe's Lake, as it is sometimes called. A resident colony of black terns enjoys swooping low over visitors who dare to enter their territory in this little wetland east of the hamlet of Eden.

Black terns are easily distinguished because they are the only members of the tern family in Manitoba with black wings. They have an active nesting colony here.

This is an important wetland for staging and breeding migratory birds. According to local historians, unpredictable water levels prompted the construction of a small stop-log water control structure located at the north end of this natural drain holding back water that forms a small marsh. Stabilized water levels contributed to healthier habitat. Patterns change, but sometimes during the spring and fall migrations large flocks of snow geese ranging upward to 15,000 birds have been recorded.

This is largely private land, but about a kilometre south is a 320-acre parcel of natural habitat. Half is owned by the local "Fish and Game" group while the remainder belongs to the local government. Visitors are welcome to enjoy their pursuit of all things natural in our world here. Walking and hiking are allowed on both without special permission.

Because the immediate area surrounding the wetland has large pastures, it is not unusual to see flocks of gray partridge or sharp-tailed grouse nearby. In early spring, if you pause to listen, you might hear the sound of ruffed grouse drumming in the nearby poplar bluffs.

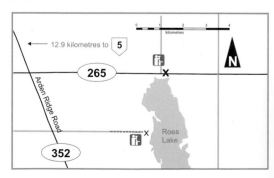

Oak Leaf

The crunching of oak leaves beneath a pair of hiking boots just might spook an inquisitive deer or draw the chattering of an agitated red squirrel. The Oak Leaf unit of the Whitemud Wildlife Management Area seldom receives visitors, but is another perfect place for one to enjoy Manitoba nature.

Often referred to as the Westlake Region, this description defines the area between Lake Manitoba and Riding Mountain National Park. This is exceptional sharp-tailed grouse and white-tailed deer habitat. It is also a great place for berry picking: saskatoons and highbush cranberries. This site is loaded with native plants, including many wildflowers, and the display changes virtually on a daily basis throughout the summer.

Oak Leaf WMA is a complex of natural habitat in a sea of agricultural development. It is situated in the aspen/oak parklands zone where prairie and aspen forest mingle, a transition between the Great Plains and the northern forest zone.

The predominant tree cover is mixed hardwood forest, primarily aspen and some bur oak. Much of this site is forest cover interspersed with meadows, which are hayed during the summer. Some of these haylands are native grasslands where during summer native wildflowers proliferate.

coyote, Dennis Weins

American goldfinch, Linda Boys

northern pearl crescent

Sightings

bobolink
whip-poor-will
warbling vireo
northern harrier
coyote

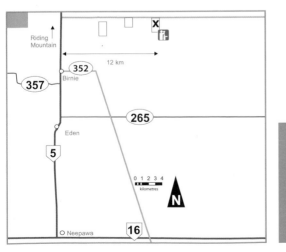

Riding Mountain

12 km

352
Birnie

357

265

Eden

5

0 1 2 3 4
kilometres
N

O Neepawa

16

From Neepawa, travel 24.5 km north on Highway 5 to the junction of PR 352. From this junction go another 6.5 km north and turn east. Unit One: Go 6.5 km east and one km south. Unit Two: return north for one km and go 1.6 km east. Unit Three: is four km east of Unit Two.

Sundance Site

great horned owl

yellow-bellied sapsucker

Sightings

coralroot
high bush cranberry
coyote
red fox
hairy woodpecker

From the junction of Highways 5 and 50 at McCreary, go 20.8 km east on Highway 50. Turn south on Glenella Road and go 9.6 km. Turn east and go 3.2 km. Turn north and go one km to the parking lot.

The Sundance Site is held in reverence by native people and it also affords exceptional opportunities to explore an area rich in natural history.

Aside from its cultural significance, this is an excellent place to learn more about the local topography, flora and fauna. The trail leading into the ritual site is lined with trembling aspen. This is a typical tree species of the region, an area defined as part of the aspen/oak parkland region; a transition where grasslands are interspersed with aspen and oak. Here, beneath the towering aspens many shade-tolerant plants grow in abundance and in the clearings native grasses and wildflowers attract a variety of butterflies and other insects.

Much of this region is considered marginal land and not really well suited for agriculture, so a great deal remains in a more natural state and adjacent lands are used as a community pasture. Even within the pasture, much of the hardwood forest remains intact, offering shelter and habitat to birds such as wren, goldfinch and warbler.

In fact the entire region provides natural treasures of significant value that are gaining attention only now. For example, showy lady's slippers, a highly sought-after threatened species, are found nearby. One extremely valuable site, lying just across Highway 50, has been identified by local naturalists as an ecologically important site worthy of protection. Efforts are underway to protect where showy

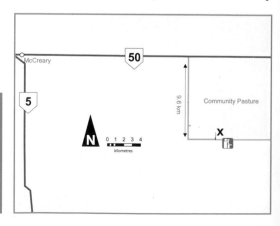

lady's slippers grow among pitcher plants and sundew, both of which are carnivorous plants.

A drive through this region in early morning or late evening rewards visitors with opportunities to see white-tailed deer, coyote, hairy woodpecker, northern flicker, red-tailed hawk, pileated woodpecker, eastern screech owl, sharp-tailed grouse and many other species of wildlife. This is truly a productive area for wildlife viewing.

This is called the "Sundance site" because it was a place used by native people to perform their traditional sun dance rituals.

Bacon Ridge Ecological Reserve

Few places can boast such an interesting resource of plant and animal life as this. The diversity is exceptional.

To some people, parts of Westlake region are considered ordinary because of the low, flat topography. But here the wildflowers are abundant in blazing colour, hawks soar, coyotes sing in the distance, and butterflies light on the dazzling prairie flowers. And locally a variety of landforms rewards explorers who venture off the main corridors. Examples are: lakeshore, tree-covered ridges, marshland and swamps.

A network of trails here demonstrates the ecological value of the forests that rim Lake Manitoba's shoreline. A trail leads through typical Westlake forest and into a black spruce swamp brimming with Labrador tea and other plants typical of a wet coniferous forest.

While "ecological reserve" forms part of the name, it was chosen to help describe the site; however, it is not officially designated as a true ecological reserve. But it is recognized by the World Wildlife Fund as a protected and endangered space due to the wildflower diversity and because of dense woods alive with neo-tropical migrant songbirds. It is an ecological treasure that should be visited and appreciated.

One of the many interesting sidebars to a visit here is the abundance of leopard frogs. They thrive close to the wet side of a lake. Wood frogs, chorus frogs and other species are also relatively abundant.

Sightings

pileated and hairy woodpecker
Wilson's warbler
chestnut-sided warbler
red-eyed vireo

From Ste. Rose du Lac, go 24 km east on Hwy. 68 to the junction of Provincial Road 278, turn and go southeast 17.6 km to the site, located on the east side of the road.

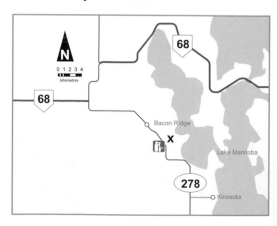

One of the cheeriest flowers here is the "prairie lily", which is always a favourite of prairie folk. Beginning in June and continuing until freeze-up, meadows come alive with wildflowers of all descriptions including another favourite, "Indian paint brush" with brilliant shades of crimson and scarlet.

indian paintbrush

Jackfish Lake

red fox, Wildlife Concepts International

Sightings

sandhill crane
American bittern
Forster's tern
American avocet
great blue heron

From Plumas, go 14.6 km east on Provincial Road 265. Turn north on the dyke, park and walk 2.5 km. Note: the dyke is not an all-weather road.

Thousands of sandhill cranes stop here during spring migration, making this one of the best places for one to observe these gangly-legged birds. As many as 6,500 sandhill cranes migrate through this area, earning the status as a North American "area-of-significance" for sandhill cranes.

Jackfish Lake, a large marshy waterbody, is part of the larger Big Grass Marsh complex. The recent nomination as a Heritage Marsh, adds to the already important-status of this world-class wetland.

Here, an amazing variety of waterfowl stages in spring, with many species staying to nest through summer. In fact, the shear diversity of bird species contributed to the area's designation as part of the Langruth Important Bird Area (IBA), an international initiative that designates areas with significant bird populations.

The Big Grass Marsh portion was determined to be critically important as a staging area for mallards and an important moulting and staging area for other waterfowl. In the past it boasted seasonal numbers of more than 200,000 snow geese and nearly 80,000 other waterfowl, bolstering its reputation as a globally important IBA. It is also recognized as having globally significant populations of nesting Franklin's gulls, estimated at more than 5,000 birds.

Jackfish Lake is the perfect location for one to explore a wetland because it is relatively accessible by "all-weather road", and offers a diversity of bird, animal and plant species.

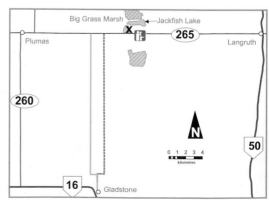

Riding Mountain

chapter 2

Biosphere Reserve

Southshore Trail, Clear Lake

McFadden Valley

Sightings

pileated and hairy woodpecker
belted kingfisher
gray jay
red-sided garter snakes
black bear

From Neepawa, travel 22 km north on Provincial Hwy. 5 and then 9.6 km west on Provincial Road 357. Then go 3.2 km north.

McFadden Valley is another stunning example of Manitoba's scenic beauty, and from the top lip of the valley looking westward the view is breathtaking. Steep valley walls and a broad, flat valley bottom combine to make this a picturesque place rich with varied plants and alive with birds and animals which enjoy the sanctuary of this valley.

The valley is a huge trench originating along the top of the Riding Mountain Escarpment, one of five segments of the Manitoba Escarpment. This segment stretches from north of Neepawa to Duck Mountain. South Snake Creek trickles along the bottom of this scenic valley. The creek's headwaters are found about ten kilometres (km) up the shale-capped escarpment. From here the valley extends south and eastward, forming a deep, wide vale, at points nearly two km across, eventually reaching a place called Big Valley.

The deep rugged gorge and valley walls provide significant habitat for one of the area's most important inhabitants, the red-sided garter snake. Many spend their winters here in the valley walls but below the frost line. The creek's name arose from the abundance of snakes.

Normally you'd expect to travel much farther north to experience a boreal forest but this region is an anomaly. At the southeast tip of Riding Mountain Escarpment you will find a boreal forest with all the plants, animals and birds that you normally associate with such

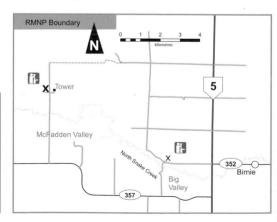

regions including gray jay, moose, elk, black bear, gray wolf and many other species.

A significant amount of Crown land is located throughout this region, making it an excellent location for walking and hiking. The area has no designated trails, so you will need a compass and a good map.

One of the best viewpoints is from the road allowance 3.2 km north of PR 357. Walk west on the undeveloped road allowance for about 0.5 km, or drive 1.6 km farther north and walk north towards the park boundary. A seasonal road leads back to Highway 5, but don't try it during wet or slippery conditions. Another scenic view is Big Valley, located to the east.

Linda Boys

Riding Mountain Biosphere Reserve

black bear, Darlene Perkin

great gray owl

indian pipe

A drive along the scenic Rolling River Tower Road is like splitting the Riding Mountain Biosphere Reserve (RMBR) in half and looking at a cross-section. The entire drive provides amazing nature moments; as wildlife, including moose, elk, and lynx are never far away. You might find unusual plants like the Indian pipe.

Stately spruce, the occasional spruce grouse and an abundance of wildflowers reward your efforts for visiting here. Two hundred and sixty species of birds have been recorded in Riding Mountain National Park (RMNP) alone, including bald eagle and osprey. Both nest here. The area is well known for its butterflies with 69 known species including 13 types of skippers.

At the Rolling River road's north end, you are in the heart of RMNP. This forms the protected core of the biosphere reserve; an area left to nature's devices where little has changed in the past 100 years.

The RMBR was designated by the United Nations Educational, Scientific and Cultural Organization (UNESCO) in 1986, and it is the only one in Manitoba. Each biosphere reserve consists of a core protected area, in this case RMNP, surrounded by a working landscape where people live and work.

As you travel, notice the thick jackpine growth, which sprouted after a huge forest fire razed the region about 25-years ago. Elk frequently cross this road and pine marten and lynx are common inhabitants. The dense

Sightings

gray wolf
lynx
black bear
spruce or ruffed grouse
boreal chickadee

From Wasagaming (Clear Lake), go five km north on Hwy 10. Turn east on Hwy. 19 and go 15.5 km to the Rolling River Tower Road. Turn south for 20 km to the junction of Provincial Road 262.

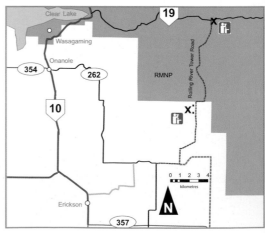

understory conceals other treasures such as the delicate Indian pipe, striped coralroot, and a vast diversity of plants.

It remains wild and rugged, although the scenery changes as you reach the park boundary. Hikers and berry pickers like it here, but fences and farming become evident. Despite limited capacity for agricultural crops, this zone forms a buffer or transition between the intensively farmed lands farther south and the protected core of the park.

Guiding, outfitting, hiking, trail riding are all sustainable activities helping to keep encroachment at bay. These activities provide income for residents, and they know it pays to protect habitat.

Keep your eyes peeled as you travel through this buffer zone, for it is an excellent area in which to see our Provincial bird, the great gray owl.

This trip nicely forms a circle tour by swinging west and back to Wasagaming or by heading south to Provincial Road 357 and then east.

To gain greater appreciation for the landscape encompassed by the RMBR, see other sites in this book including the Trans Canada Trail at Sandy Lake, Elk Glen, Skene's Crossing, Aspen Parkland and McFadden Valley.

Kerr's Lake

Trans Canada Trail — Sandy Lake

American goldfinch

Sightings

white-tailed deer
ducks
warbler
American goldfinch

Start in Sandy Lake on Provincial Road 250 and go west on the TCT. (To reach Jackfish Lake, from the junction of Highway 10 and 45, go 6.8 km west and then go 1.4 km north to the TCT. Park and walk west.)

A thick, lush understory graces the forest lining the trail, harbouring birds and other creatures beneath the swaying aspens. The trail runs along the south shore of Beaufort Lake, allowing access for hikers and bikers interested in enjoying the sights and sounds of nature in a tranquil rural setting.

Listen as you pass by the aspen stand, the shaking sounds from an otherwise peaceful forest clearly illustrate why these trees are known as "trembling aspen".

Another place to access the trail is found near Jackfish Lake. Here, beneath the aspens, the dense understory is rich with chokecherry, saskatoon, asters, fleabane and goldenrod; an interesting mix. Butterflies, songbirds and insects thrive in this part of the forest.

On the forest floor the grasses appear empty until the "throaty-clucking-sound" of a wood frog penetrates the air. With careful observation and a lot of patience, you might notice a slight movement from the frog's hiding spot. He's not alone here; the forest floor is actually home to plenty of creatures from the tiny ants and other insects to the cottontail rabbits that make their living in the winter, nipping the ends of branches. Their tiny incisors prune the shrubs, causing them to bush out with results similar to those of people tending their houseplants.

Another forest layer, the canopy, is the roof where the crowns of tall trees compete for the sun's direct light. This, a segment of the Trans Canada Trail (TCT), starts at Neepawa and

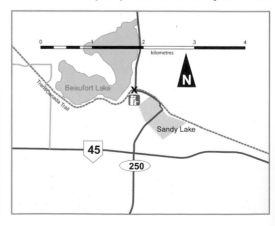

extends for 190 km to Russell. This feature is representative of the entire trail's length, although it changes with each kilometre from start to finish. This point is within the Riding Mountain Biosphere Reserve.

These trails are valuable because they form a cross-section stretching for kilometres allowing us a convenient way to see the inside of the forest and brush and leading along the edges of lakes, sloughs, marshes and other features. In fact, the scattering of sloughs and small lakes teaming with waterfowl and other wildlife are one of the trail's many highlights.

Listen for the familiar quacking sounds of dabbling ducks — like a mallard — or the cheerful song of warbler or finch. At other points, the forest gives way to openings and you can enjoy scenic prairie vistas. You might be lucky enough to see a herd of deer grazing in an alfalfa field or coyote hunting for mice in the tall grass.

weasel

Elk Glen

This isn't typical prairie landscape by any stretch of your imagination. Inch for inch, Elk Glen is one of the most rugged parts of Manitoba that you are likely to encounter anywhere.

Located just outside the south boundary of Riding Mountain National Park, the surrounding country roads and hilltops present majestic scenery with breathtaking views. Further east, a hilltop known locally as "Cranberry Hill" towers high over the other peaks along the Riding Mountain Escarpment.

As the name implies, elk frequent this spot and the surrounding countryside, in addition to moose, gray wolves, coyote, owls, and a variety of other birds and animals you would normally expect to find in a boreal forest or mixed-wood forest setting.

Its close proximity to the Park provides this spot with many benefits for wildlife-viewing because the park acts as a refuge allowing wildlife to spill out beyond its boundaries into Elk Glen and the surrounding countryside.

This unusual and rugged landscape makes it one of the most unique places to visit in the entire province. Currently Elk Glen, covering 802-acres, is owned by the Nature Conservancy of Canada (NCC). However, local residents have hammered a trail through Elk Glen, sticking close to the otherwise undeveloped road allowance running east/west through the centre. While designed as a snowmobile trail it doubles as a hiking trail, although not marked or maintained for that purpose. Other than snowmobiles, motorized traffic is not permitted here.

Sightings

red-tailed hawk
elk
black bear
pileated woodpecker

From Rossburn, go 19 km north on PR 264. Where the road turns, park and walk 1.2 km east to Elk Glen. Cranberry Hill is reached by going 12 km north from Rossburn and then east on the municipal road. Ask for directions locally for this leg of the journey.

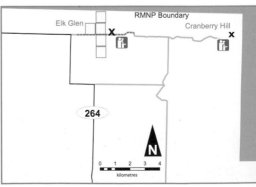

Other trails criss-cross, providing access opportunities and making this an excellent way to visit and explore depths of Elk Glen. Enjoy the surroundings and appreciate the dramatic changes in elevation, the panoramic views, succulent vegetation, prolific wildlife and the best that nature has to offer. But exercise caution, as these trails are not maintained and there are very steep inclines.

This location is part of the Riding Mountain Biosphere Reserve, the only biosphere reserve in Manitoba. See the RMBR site in this book for more details.

Aspen Parkland

downy woodpecker

Ryan Brook

From Dauphin, go 45 km west on Hwy. 5 to Grandview and turn south on Provincial Road 366 and go 11 km. When PR 366 turns west, continue south for 6.4 km, then stop and walk along the park boundary. To make this into a circle tour, return to PR 366 and drive west to PR 584 and north to Hwy. 5.

The Riding Mountain elk is without question the "Prince" of the region's forests. Imagine a massive bull elk, antlers tossed back and breath steaming from his nostrils. This is undeniably one of the most exhilarating nature experiences imaginable! Patches of aspen are in a way similar to "giant stepping stones," connecting Riding Mountain National Park to the Duck Mountain area.

Elk, like white-tailed deer, moose, bear, gray wolves and even some songbirds, instinctively migrate between the two large habitat reserves, using these islands of habitat to narrow the distance and limit their time in open country.

Recently the Nature Conservancy of Canada (NCC) has been working with landowners in the area to secure and protect these valuable patches of habitat through Conservation Agreements, also known as easements.

To gain appreciation for this remarkable landscape, drive toward the park boundary and then look north for a bird's eye view of the distant Duck Mountain.

Stop and walk along the park boundary where you may hear the drumming of grouse, the pounding of woodpeckers and the cheerful chorus of songbirds. Just inside the park you will notice birch clumps mixed with the aspen. This habitat mix provides plenty of shelter for wildlife.

Two of the province's most valued elk herds are found near this site, one in Riding Mountain and the other in Duck Mountain.

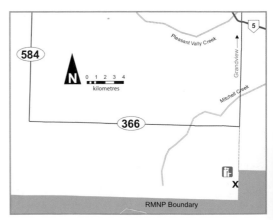

Recent studies clearly show a relationship between the two herds and proof that the elk move between the two regions. The bond that these two herds share is this stretch of Aspen Parkland that joins these two reservoirs of habitat.

Parkland is a term normally used to classify a geographic region that forms the transition between the prairie and the boreal forest. This entire region is a rich mosaic of aspen forest in association with other hardwoods and interspersed with a variety of habitat including grasslands, potholes and small wetlands. This is one of our most threatened habitat types because they are often selected for agriculture.

NCC is making a real difference to our natural environment. To learn more about their involvement, visit these sites in this book: Elk Glen, Yellow Quill, Agassiz Trail, Jiggens Bluff and Pembina Valley Provincial Park.

Milbert's tortoise shell

Skene's Crossing

tall coneflower

Jack Ganzel

Sightings

white-tailed deer
turkey vulture
horned owl
coyote
northern leopard frog

From Dauphin, go 24 km southeast on Hwy. 20. Cross Hwy. 5 and go south eight km on Provincial Road 582. Go east about 1.6 km and turn south. Go about 5.4 km south, turn west and go about 3.4 km to a scenic viewpoint overlooking the crossing. Continue farther and take the first gravel road northwest to the crossing.

It is a safe bet that visitors will be pleasantly surprised by the uniqueness and scenic beauty here. Nothing else across the province compares with these lush banks, flat rock-bottomed river beds and scenic vistas along this part of the Ochre River.

After heavy rains and spring run-off, torrential floodwater spills down the Riding Mountain Escarpment. Rushing water scours the streambeds, recharging the Ochre River in the process as it cascades down the hillside through deeply carved valleys and gorges along the way. Elevations change dramatically between the top of the escarpment and the flat farmlands in the distance. One of the best points from which to view and explore this landscape is at the place local people call "Skene's Crossing", a plateau-like spot part way down the escarpment.

At the "crossing", the river is wide with a solid bottom, perfect for exploring. In both directions there are exposed shale banks.

There is plenty of Crown land in all directions from the crossing where the public has open access to explore on foot and experience the wild side of Manitoba. Just south of the crossing is a tract of land owned by the Manitoba Habitat Corporation. It was set aside to protect the ecological integrity of a very productive piece of habitat where white-tailed deer, turkey vultures, horned owls, and coyotes are all common.

Check at the local municipal office to determine the Crown land locations.

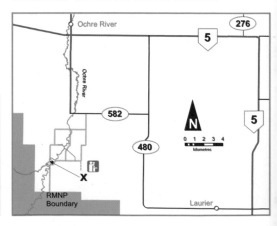

Assiniboine River

Willms Unit

prairie coneflower

When the prairie sun begins to set in the west, a glorious golden hue transforms the prairie landscape into a postcard scene. A mallard with its wings set glides effortlessly into a prairie pothole and the song of a distant meadowlark can be heard.

This tranquil scene may not be as serene as it appears. A hungry fox lurks in the tall grass, hoping that an unsuspecting vole will join him for dinner — his, not the vole's, that is! A striped skunk is also on the prowl, hunting for duck eggs. These natural processes apply here in this healthy, vibrant prairie ecosystem.

Potholes are the lifeblood for many species of prairie waterfowl, yet these willow-rimmed sloughs are surrounded with upland cover that is critical for many ground-nesting ducks.

As much as 70 percent of all Manitoba's wildlife clings to the thread of life in the agricultural region of the province. Willms is typical of habitat in farmland where wildlife often thrives in relative harmony with crop production.

The sloughs and aspen bluffs are interspersed with remnants of native prairie that have managed to survive undisturbed. The difference between these and other patches of native grasses is the diversity and abundance of native grassland species such as spear grass, harebell, giant-hyssop and others.

The Willms property consists of 320 acres of critical wildlife habitat, purchased to ensure representative areas of native grasses and prairie potholes remain for future generations.

This site has potholes, a creek, a small reservoir created by a small dam, aspen bluffs, tree plantations, dense nesting cover and much more. Each one of these habitat types is home to a variety of plants and wildlife, including reptiles and butterflies.

Sightings

raccoon
Le Conte's sparrow
western meadowlark
savannah sparrow
common yellowthroat

From Brandon, go north 14 km from the Junction of Highways 1 and 10. At the Junction of Highways 10 and 25 turn east and travel 6.4 km, to reach the southwest corner of the property.

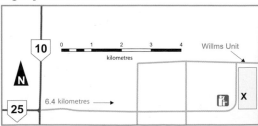

Picturing this place the way it must have been prior to European settlement is easy; time has changed little here. For literally as far as the eye can see, prairie grasses bend to the wind, intricately blending with the yellow-tipped red blossoms of gaillardia, the blues of harebells, the purple of blazing star, and many other plants and flowers on one of the best remaining "nearly-intact" tracts of mixed grass prairie.

This is exactly what the Great Plains must have looked like hundreds of years ago. Native prairie remains on the adjoining lands as well.

Large tracts of mixed-grass prairie are increasingly rare, as a result of agriculture and other development. Mixed-grass prairie was the transition between the tall-grass prairie of the Red River region and the short-grass prairie farther west.

At Rivers, about 120 acres of native prairie are formally protected. The prairie grasses, speckled with wildflowers, wave in the late summer sun while hawks drift overhead and a V-shaped flock of geese skirt the north shore of Lake Wahtopanah nearby. The lake is a reservoir on the Little Saskatchewan River, an ancient glacial spillway, characterized by high, rolling hills.

The patches of "undisturbed" native prairie have never met the plough and are easily discerned from other patches of grass by the diversity of native plant species. These include big bluestem, Indian breadroot and harebell.

This area is thought to have cultural significance, for stones found here may be petroforms, which are ancient forms shaped using rocks. These have not been authenticated.

crocus

Dennis Wiens

Sightings

gaillardia
mixed grass prairie
vesper sparrow
savannah sparrow
mountain bluebird
sharp-tailed grouse

From Rivers, go 0.8 km north on Provincial Road 250. Turn east and go 2.4 km.

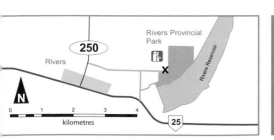

Pope National Wildlife Area

greater yellowlegs

Sightings

gadwall,
ruddy duck
pied-billed grebe
raccoon
weasel
coyote

From Brandon, go 25 km north on Highway 10. Turn west and go 50 km on Highway 24. Go 3.2 km south on Highway 21. Turn west for 5.6 km.

It surprises many people to learn that Manitoba is home to two of only a handful of National Wildlife Areas in our entire nation. Even more surprising is that this national reserve is nestled in a sleepy hollow between Oakner and Hamiota, an area that at first glance might not appear to harbour important habitat. Manitoba's other NWA is in the Interlake near Gunton.

Farm country is where the majority of Manitoba's wildlife is found. Idle road allowances, fencelines, shelterbelts, potholes, bluffs, coulees and other habitat normally interspersed with cultivated land, provide cover and travel corridors.

Known locally as Strachan Slough, this is the deepest waterbody in a region covered with small lakes, prairie potholes and sloughs. Pope is located in a prime waterfowl production region; characterized by a multitude of wetlands separated by farmland.

Dating back as far as 1966, water from this reservoir was used to help regulate Bars Lakes marsh complex, found about six km south of Pope NWA.

The reservoir was created when an earthen dam was constructed in 1926, forming a deep wetland providing a secure source of water for steam engines. The deep water attracts waterfowl, especially in dry years as this is sometimes the only place where it remains. But even in wet years, Pope shows its worth as a loafing and staging area for all types of ducks, and nesting habitat for many.

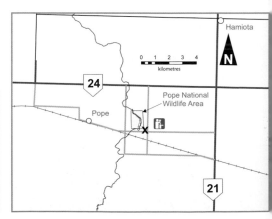

A walk along the muddy shores shows good use by white-tailed deer, raccoon, mink and other wildlife which leave their footprints in the moist soil for visitors to interpret.

Pope is a tiny area, covering only 77 acres including a narrow band of riparian cover, or green zone, surrounding the open water. The adjacent land is privately owned. Pubic access is restricted to the road allowance on the south and west ends and a narrow belt of public land.

Nearby, Bars Lake is a series of ponds, sloughs and improved wetlands that combine to provide roughly 450-acres of habitat that plays an important waterfowl production role. It is also important for muskrats and other marsh wildlife. The surrounding uplands contain good examples of mixed grass prairie; remnants from a time prior to development.

raccoon

Niso Valley

yellow-bellied sapsucker

Sightings

red-eyed vireo
American redstart
hairy woodpecker
red-sided garter snake
least flycatcher
white-tailed deer

From Miniota, go 3.2 km south on Provincial Highway 83. After crossing the river, turn and go 1.2 km west and 1.5 km south.

Who says the prairies are flat? A visit to the spectacular Niso Valley, one of the prairie's true gems, proves otherwise.

Just off Highway 83, visitors are afforded spectacular views, especially in autumn as the hardwoods turn to orange and yellow in contrast to late-turning leaves that linger green, and the brilliant red of shrubs such as the highbush cranberry.

The view of the valley where Niso Creek cuts through the landscape before joining the Assiniboine River is breath-taking. The Assiniboine meanders eastward, eventually joining with the Red River at the Forks in Winnipeg.

Steep drops, actually more like cliffs in some cases, characterize this gem. One of the best views is from the Reeder Unit of the Upper Assiniboine Wildlife Management Area (WMA) found southwest of Miniota. A municipal road snakes up the steep valley leading to a terrific vantage point on the valley's crest. A wide variety of unmarked trails are accessible from this road and they wind along the valley edge, leading visitors through the wildlife area and the public land where hikers and berry pickers are welcome.

This is one of the many small wildlife areas set aside throughout this region.

The entire 750-acre WMA is alive with wildlife of all types and sizes ranging from the smallest insects and butterflies to coyotes and white-tailed deer.

In spring and fall, red-sided garter snakes

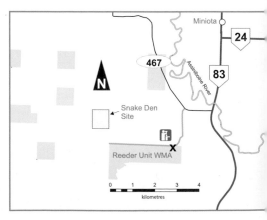

slither across the roads and trails. In fall, they head back to their dens in the base of the valley slopes to the west, where they hibernate below the frost-line during winter. These winter snake dens are one of the most important sites of this nature in the province.

Niso Creek and this region's most dominant feature, the Assiniboine River Valley, were created by melting glaciers. This explains why there is a small river channel in the bottom of a huge river valley. Floodwaters from the melting ice sheet carved massive river valleys through much of this region.

Many migrant neo-tropical birds use this river valley as travel corridors.

Lidcliff Marsh

Shorebirds love Lidcliff Marsh because of the exposed saline flats which provide them with feeding and resting areas. These flats attract marbled godwit, willet, American avocet and many other shorebirds. This is also one of the better sites for viewing great blue and black-crowned night heron and to find an eared grebe colony. The marsh is a major production and moulting area for canvasbacks and redheads.

About 1,360-acres are currently owned by the Manitoba Wildlife Federation Habitat Foundation Inc., a non-profit conservation group. Their land is open to the public for nature observations, photography and other outdoor pursuits.

Actually, Lidcliff isn't a single marsh; rather it is a complex of several wetlands. In wet years, much of the marsh is under water and smaller areas merge. In dry years, from a "duck's-eye-view", it appears more like a series of puddles joined by grasslands.

These grasslands provide excellent cover for ground-nesting waterfowl and shorebirds. In spring and autumn, this marsh is an important staging area for migrating waterfowl. Adjoining upland areas are important for sharp-tailed grouse.

This area is historically important for muskrat production but their numbers have declined from their peak in the 1940's.

This entire wetland is now designated as a candidate Heritage Marsh under the Manitoba Heritage Marsh Program.

Sightings

Wilson's phalarope
migrant shorebirds
American avocet
muskrat
mallard

From Russell, go 19 km south on Highway 16, turn east and go 13.6 km.

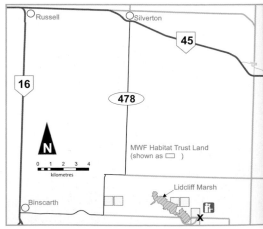

Southwest chapter 4

Riverside

Bunclody

Linda Boys

Sightings

Swainson's hawk
great blue heron
wood duck
mountain and eastern bluebird
white-tailed deer

From Brandon, go 24 km south on Highway 10. Turn west for seven km on Provincial Highway 2 and then go 9.5 km south on a gravel road to reach the Souris River.

Riverside: From Brandon, go 39 km south on Highway 10. The view west overlooks the WMA.

The deep blue waters of the meandering Souris River combine with the crisp green vegetation buffering the stream providing a gorgeous scenic viewpoint at Bunclody.

The Souris River enters Manitoba from North Dakota south of Melita and eventually empties into the Assiniboine River. Along the way it provides many scenic vistas and wildlife viewing opportunities including this accessible and scenic point from the Bunclody Bridge.

Nearby, a small wayside park makes a perfect picnic site. The surrounding municipal roads are available for hikes, and walking where you can enjoy nature at your own pace.

The riparian area bordering the Souris River is an excellent example of riverbottom deciduous forest harbouring a variety of bird and animal species.

Along the river, tree species here include bur oak, aspen and Manitoba maple. Grasslands, riparian area and deep river valley with wooded and semi-open valley slopes provide plenty of diversity. As a result you may find a good variety of bird species from spring migration, throughout the nesting season and fall migration. These could include: clay-coloured sparrow, eastern phoebe, Baltimore oriole, catbird, eastern towhee, eastern and mountain bluebird and many others.

Bunclody provides a scenic vista, but this is a sample of the adventure awaiting visitors along this tree-lined stream. About two km northwest, a 640-acre tract of Crown land is available for the more adventuresome to explore, but it is in a natural state with difficult access and no services. About four km southeast lies the rugged Riverside Wildlife Management Area, with a scenic view found along Highway 10.

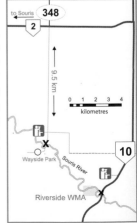

Sexton's Island

Tundra swans skimming low over the marsh, strung out in long, loosely-formed V-shapes pass directly over Sexton's Island. These large white birds, wings beating rhythmically, slowly gain altitude before reaching the farm fields just beyond the marsh's boundaries. Tundra swans are usually plentiful during spring migration.

A marsh in the most traditional sense, this area is rich in both plant and animal life. Sexton's Island is one of many particularly productive places along the north shore of this shallow waterbody known as Whitewater Lake. This is a massive expanse of wetland, encompassing about 29,600 acres with tremendous ecological significance. The Island takes up about 220-acres of the lake.

Large expanses of open water in the middle are ringed by marsh vegetation surrounded by haylands and meadows. Beyond that, to the north stretch the agricultural lands, which are interspersed with aspen bluffs.

This is considered to be one of the continent's most significant wetlands and it has always attracted massive numbers of waterfowl during the spring and fall migrations.

The lake is a closed, shallow, alkaline wetland and is a very important staging area for waterfowl, shorebirds, and extremely popular with songbirds of all descriptions. Sexton's Island is just one spot in this unique habitat, but it adds great diversity to the Whitewater Lake basin — from open water,

black-crowned night heron, V. Jackson

Sightings

tundra swan
sandhill crane
Franklin's gull
black tern
northern harrier
red fox

From Brandon, take Highway 10 south for 47 km, turn west for 18 km on Provincial Highway 23 and south on PR 448 for 16.5 km. Turn west for 3 km, and then turn south. Park and walk two km to Sexton's Island. **Viewing mound: From Boissevain,** go 6 km south. Turn west on Hwy 3, go 11 km west and follow the signs.

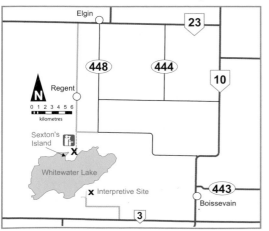

Elgin · 23 · 448 · 444 · 10 · Regent · 0 1 2 3 4 5 6 kilometres · N · Sexton's Island · X · Whitewater Lake · X Interpretive Site · 443 · Boissevain · 3

emergent marsh, wet meadow, Mixed Grass Prairie to oak and maple woods.

In spring it is a major breeding and nesting area. Recent noteworthy observations include cattle egret, white-faced ibis, western grebe, white-rumped sandpiper, trumpeter swan, sandhill crane, ferruginous hawk, and American avocet. More than 250 bird species have been identified here, however the diversity of the lake is not limited to birds, as it provides habitat for many other wildlife species and vegetation types.

Besides being a provincial wildlife management area, this wetland is also nominated as a heritage marsh; a designation reserved for the most productive wetlands. More recently it was listed as a "globally significant" Important Bird Area (IBA).

An IBA is a location designated as globally important habitat for the conservation of bird populations.

At least eight different bird species meet the IBA criteria as globally significant here, including the Franklin's Gull, sometimes found here in numbers ranging up to 30,000. The black-crowned night heron meets the nationally significant criteria, with up to 85 breeding pairs.

The access trail is rough and during periods of high water, it may be flooded. As an alternative, visit the southeast corner of the marsh, which contains a viewing mound, boardwalk and interpretive signage.

Whitewater Lake

Chain Lakes

On a warm fall evening, small flocks of lesser scaup ducks come down the long valley, with wings beating rapidly as they pass overhead; their formations shift from waving lines to temporary V's. A few seconds later they disappear into the blazing red sunset over Chain Lakes.

This is an unusual, magnificent tract consisting of three small lakes in a beautiful natural valley setting and a much overlooked attraction. During migration, waterfowl numbers swell as scaup, canvasbacks, redheads, mallards and other ducks drop in just before dark. Some spend their days foraging for feed in surrounding cropland, then return to the lakes for the night.

The easiest public access is made from Highway 21 along Chain Lakes Road. This is a good all weather road which takes you right down near the water's edge between two of three lakes. Remember to stick to the road allowances or ask for landowner's permission.

These lakes are small and hiking is the best way to view birds and animals. Although a bit difficult in places, it is possible to walk portions of shoreline. The central lake is a bit larger in size than the other two.

White-tailed deer numbers fluctuate significantly in this locale, but they are always relatively common. Back roads in the surrounding farm country make excellent places for an evening drive to view wildlife.

It is equally rewarding to find a vantage point on one of the hilltops along the valley. Pause here, listen carefully for late arriving flocks of ducks whistling over the hilltops before they drop to the lake for the night. Or sit and watch the most amazing sunsets, especially during autumn when the sky will often fill with flocks of waterfowl.

Anita Brabyk

Sightings

white-tailed deer
willow flycatcher
chestnut-collared longspur
ferruginous hawk
eared grebe

From Hartney, travel 12 km south on Highway 21, and follow the gravel road east for 1.2 km, turn south and go one km.

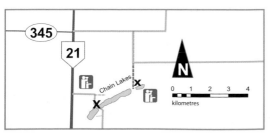

Blind Souris

Dave McArthur

Sightings

upland sandpiper
Sprague's pipit
Baird's sparrow
ferruginous hawk
jackrabbit

From Melita, go 13 km south on Highway 83 and five km east. This takes you into the valley where you can begin to explore on your own between here and Melita and south to Coulter.

The valley bottom is stunning and a virtual treasure-trove full of unusual plants and interesting wildlife. Blind Souris isn't a specific location, rather it is a grasslands area bordering a lengthy expanse of dry creek bed. This is one of the most interesting locations you are likely to encounter as you explore rural southwestern Manitoba's diverse landscape.

The Souris River is a landmark dominating the southwest corner of the province. This was not always the case. Hundreds of years ago another mighty river flowed across the southwest from the North Dakota Border, joining the Souris River near Melita.

Likely as a result of the continent rebounding after the glaciers melted following the last ice age, the Blind Souris gradually stopped its continuous flow. Today it is roughly described as a region starting near Coulter, then extending north to Melita.

The waters may have slowed, but the value for wildlife and native plants has not ebbed. Among the most important natural spaces we have, it provides ideal conditions for several species at risk including Baird's sparrow, Sprague's pipit and ferruginous hawk. It is also one of the last remaining areas where buffalograss occurs in the province.

Buffalograss, as the name implies, was a favourite food of the bison herds that once roamed these mixed-grass prairies. Today, like the bison, they are virtually gone.

In his book "Birds of Manitoba", Ernest Thompson Seton wrote that Baird's sparrow was once found throughout southern Manitoba referring to it as "one of the commonest birds." Today, Baird's sparrow is restricted to suitable habitat in the extreme southwestern corner including the Blind Souris.

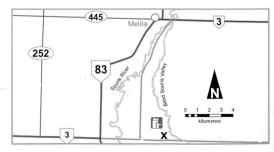

Canupawakpa Trail

Canupawakpa Trail might best be described as the "Jewel of the Pipestone". Here the story of the riparian zone's importance unfolds, as Pipestone Creek snakes its way through a riverbottom forest, surrounded by the sights and sounds of a tranquil country setting.

Indigenous people have long used Pipestone Creek for transportation and for camping sites. The name, Canupawakpa, is a Sioux word meaning Pipe River, earned from a peace pipe found here in 1876.

This valley was born some 14,000 years ago as a result of melting glaciers that formed glacial Lake Regina. Escaping melt waters formed the valley and shaped the surrounding region.

Riparian refers to the green belt along the edges of rivers, lakes and sloughs. These areas make up less than five percent of our landscape, yet 80 percent of all our wildlife depends on them as habitat. A healthy riparian area, like this one, is usually more succulent than the adjoining uplands. Plants enjoy the added moisture while the lush vegetation provides food and shelter that attracts wildlife.

If you want to slow your pace, this serene river trail offers a chance to take a closer look at the smaller creatures and plants that might be otherwise overlooked.

Stop and listen; you may hear the "peeping" sound of the chorus frog that is often found here. Also common is the wood frog; you will recognize him by the bandit's mask he wears. Look in the trees, as hollow trunks often conceal nesting birds, or other creatures.

An interesting aspect of the trail is the variety of wild plants including several edible kinds. For example; pin cherry, wild plum, saskatoon, raspberry and chokecherry are all here.

red squirrel

Pipestone Creek

Sightings

rose-breasted grosbeak
yellow-throated vireo
warbling vireo
least flycatcher
great crested flycatcher

From Reston, go 1.2 km east on Highway 2 and 2.4 km north.

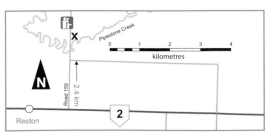

Jiggen's Bluff

gaillardia

eared grebe

Sightings

lobelia
short-eared owl
Le Conte's sparrow
sedge wren
weasel

From Souris, go 28 km west on Highway 2. Turn north on PR 254 for 3.5 km.

Any plant or wildlife enthusiast will love a hike through the conservation agency land at this site. It consists of three main cover types: grassy meadows, tree covered hummocky hills and marsh; each with its own array of native plants for visitors' enjoyment. The name, Jiggen's Bluff, is derived because of the wooded hills here, and includes the surrounding area.

Along the main entrance road, near the east side of this expansive tract of habitat, open fields are brightly carpeted with wildflowers in July and August, attracting plenty of butterflies and other insects.

Farther west, the rolling hills add interesting relief to the area characterized by oak dominated mixed-forest interspersed with meadows. These woods and glades are home to a wide variety of birds and animals.

Several small sloughs are located along the roads at the east end of Jiggen's Bluff. As well, a significant wetland stretches across the entire southern limits. In wet years it takes on the appearance of a small lake while in drier years it is much more marsh-like in appearance. This is excellent waterfowl nesting habitat. Different types of hawks are frequently seen here, or heard screeching in the distance.

Throughout the surrounding hinterlands you may see a variety of interesting birds including Sprague's pipit, chestnut-collared longspur, American bittern and short-eared owl.

There is easy access to the grasslands on the east side, but the bluff is not accessible. Initially large portions of land were purchased by the Nature Conservancy of Canada, and later transferred to Ducks Unlimited. These lands, plus Crown land and road allowances are available for visitors.

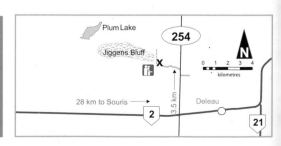

Devil's Punch Bowl

Yellow Quill and Criddle-Vane

red-tailed hawk

Sightings

Sprague's pipit
sharp-tailed grouse
red-tailed hawk
purple prairie clover
rare plants such as sand bluestem

From Shilo, go 10 km south on Provincial Road 340. Turn east and go 3.2 km to the Criddle / Vane Homestead Provincial Heritage Park. Turn south and go 3.2 km and then 1.6 km east to the Yellow Quill Prairie.

Walk to the middle of the Yellow Quill Prairie and stand still. Listen as a red-tailed hawk screeches overhead and watch the prairie grasses bobbing in the wind; let your imagination wander, taking you to another time. You can almost hear the excited voices of the Criddle and Vane children making their way to the Assiniboine River through what was then a near-endless sea of flower-laden prairie grasses.

Today only small remnants of native prairie remain, although this important habitat is still bound to impress visitors with its scenic beauty.

The Criddle/Vane family arrived in 1882 and enjoyed the surrounding landscape brimming with wildflowers, other plants and wildlife throughout this sandy region. In the years that followed they carefully identified and documented hundreds of insect and plant species.

Recently the family homestead was designated as a "Provincial Park" and recognized as a unique contribution to Manitoba's natural heritage, due to the diversity of plants and animals found here.

One of the best places to enjoy our natural heritage, reminiscent of the early days, is to visit the nearby Yellow Quill Prairie with its expanse of native mixed-grass prairie, much of which was once owned by the Criddle family.

Each spring the prairie comes to life providing a constant display of wildflowers

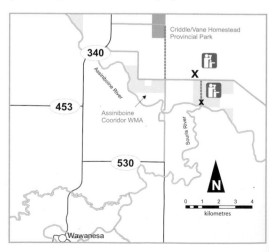

and other native plants that continually change from early spring until freeze up. The prairie crocus is among the earliest flowers emerging from the cold soil. With brilliant blue and purple hues, it is followed by yellow lady's slippers, harebells and other flowers each unleashing its own unique beauty.

Take time to enjoy the prairie and surrounding countryside. The Yellow Quill Prairie consists of 2,080 acres which, together with the Criddle/Vane Provincial Park and the Assiniboine River Corridor Wildlife Management Area (WMA), combine to make an amazing treasure.

A walk across the WMA provides a panoramic view of the spectacular Assiniboine River near the historic junction of the Souris River.

If you approach cautiously, you may see a mallard hen with her brood or catch a glimpse of a raccoon scouring the river for clams or other food.

The Yellow Quill Prairie Project is owned by the Nature Conservancy of Canada, a national organization dedicated to the conservation of ecologically significant land through private action, and to its long-term stewardship through monitoring and management agreements with landowners.

Here a mixture of prairie grasses interspersed with aspen bluffs grow on sandy land that is home to a wide diversity of common and rare mixed-grass prairie plants. Some of the more rare plants include the red three-awned grass and sand bluestem.

This is home to a wealth of wildlife that presents itself at its will, for our enjoyment. A curious coyote or fox, American badger, deer, elk and Swainson's hawk are but a few of the species that a watchful eye may detect.

prickly-pear cactus

S-Lake

purple coneflower

northern pearl crescent

Sightings

alder flycatcher
marsh wren
broad-winged hawk
northern harrier
purple coneflower

From Ninette, go 4.8 km north on Highway 18. Turn west and go 10 km and turn north for one km.

Gaillardia and purple coneflowers sway in the wind along the long sloping valley walls that stretch across this broad valley. Unknowingly, you might guess you were some other place far removed from Manitoba.

S-Lake is a name given to the location where the lake is found. The property covers 320-acres of Crown land held in the name of the Manitoba Habitat Heritage Corporation and dedicated to the memory of Richard C. Goulden, who will long be remembered as one of Manitoba's most noteworthy habitat managers. What better place to commemorate a conservationist than a place teeming with wildlife and providing a broad range of environmental benefits spilling out well beyond the property's boundaries.

This is the extreme northwest end of the Pembina River drainage system, and, in fact forms the divide between the Pembina and the Souris River systems.

Only a few kilometres east is Bone Lake, a small natural lake that augments the habitat values of S-Lake, and provides some of the most breathtaking sunsets imaginable! Beyond that is Pelican Lake, Southern Manitoba's largest waterbody.

The top of this valley is crested with bur oak, maple, green ash and paper birch. While the hillsides slope towards the valley bottom, they are regularly interrupted with coulees. These are small dry ravines colonized by chokecherry, beaked hazelnut and other shrubs. This forms a criss-cross pattern along the valley's entire length. Between these, lie patches of grassland that are home to gray partridge, and countless other varieties of wildlife.

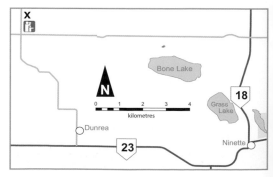

When a half-ton moose clears its nostrils twenty metres away, it is enough to raise the hairs on the back of your neck!

Viewing North America's largest member of the deer family up "close and personal" is one of the most exhilarating experiences outdoor enthusiasts are ever likely to have, and nowhere are your chances of seeing a moose better than at the International Peace Garden.

Many people often mistakenly think the Peace Garden, located along the edge of Turtle Mountain Provincial Park, as simply the gateway to the USA, while others view it as a beautiful flower garden, towering nearly 200-metres above the surrounding plains. While both ideas are true, this is not the only attraction this park-like setting holds. It also offers world-class wildlife viewing.

The mixed-wood forests, interspersed with marshland and lakes are habitat for moose and other wildlife. Because the area is a refuge, although totally wild, it us one of the most accessible moose viewing opportunities in the province.

But the Peace Garden's nature viewing opportunities aren't limited to moose. Although this is far from the north, the common loon is abundant and highly visible on the small lakes here.

The lake along the Lakeview Hiking Trail, located in the north portion of the park, is an excellent spot to hear and see loons, the icon of Manitoba's north and wilderness areas.

About 100 different species of songbirds have been identified in the vicinity including: Baltimore oriole, black-and-white warbler and the mountain bluebird.

Darlene Perkin

Sightings

moose
white-tailed deer
common loon
indigo bunting
great-crested flycatcher
red-eyed vireo

From Boissevain, go 27 km south on Highway 10 and one km west.

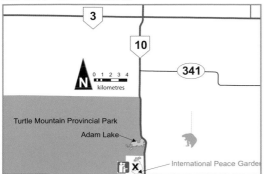

3

10

341

N
0 1 2 3 4
kilometres

Turtle Mountain Provincial Park

Adam Lake

International Peace Garden

Lorne Lake

Nestled deep within an oak-rimmed valley, this "Pretty as a Postcard" tiny lake attracts little attention, but its shores harbour a vast storehouse of wildlife and plenty of scenery.

This prairie gem is within the Pembina Valley, between Pelican and Rock Lake.

The southeast corner of the lake is picturesque, nestled amid the hardwood forest, dominated by oak and aspen, but including birch, ash and other tree species. The northwest shoreline of Lorne Lake is protected within the West Derby Unit of the Pembina Valley Wildlife Management Area. Here 320-acres of Crown land are available for one to explore; however, there is limited access except along the southern extent of this WMA.

Getting to Lorne Lake is half the fun! If you approach from the tiny community of Neelin, you will be traversing one of the most picturesque stretches of landscape found anywhere along the western reaches of the Pembina escarpment. Steep valley walls, scenic vistas and winding roads make the drive to Lorne Lake doubly delightful! You'll also glimpse an assortment of wildlife that freely ranges the area. A variety of songbirds are particularly plentiful here through the nesting and migration season. Hawks, owls, wild turkey and white-tailed deer are also here at times.

Sightings

red-headed woodpecker
rose-breasted grosbeak
indigo bunting
Baltimore oriole

From Baldur, go six km west on Highway 23. Turn south on Highway 5 and go 19 km. Go through the Town of Neelin, jog north and then continue west for 4.8 km.

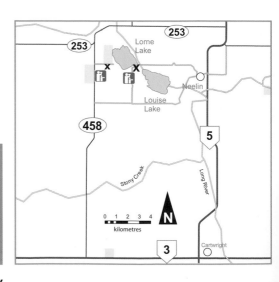

Assiniboine South – Trans Canada Trail

A lengthy trail snakes across North America, reaching from coast to coast. In Manitoba the Trans Canada Trail winds through some of our province's most exciting and diverse regions including Spruce Woods Provincial Park.

One of the most interesting segments of the trail runs north from Cypress River through the sandhills and passes near the "Hogs Back", a remarkable, yet often overlooked natural feature. The trail then swings west alongside the mighty Assiniboine River, eventually reaching Highway 5.

The park is a dominant feature in south-central Manitoba with a well deserved reputation for scenery that earned its status as a major attraction. Outstanding features include the Spirit Sands, also known as a "living desert" and the oasis-like feature known as the Devil's Punch Bowl; but these are just two of the special attractions.

One of the lesser known features is the "Hog's Back". This razorback ridge is separated from the feature's trail head by a gorgeous bowl-shaped valley where beavers have created a pond that further enhances the image. The ridge resembles a "hog's back", giving rise to the name. A short trail leads visitors along the Hog's Back, and the trailhead and the ridge are roughly the same height. Between the two is a beautiful scenic bowl that was carved by erosion. As stunning as this site may be, it is not well known.

prairie skink

Sightings

prickly-pear cactus
pink-flowered onion
indigo bunting
broad-winged hawk
turkey vulture

From Cypress River, go 1.5 km east on Highway 2. Turn north on Park Road and go 11 km to where the Trans Canada Trail branches off to the west. To reach the Hog's Back, continue north three km, turn east and follow the signs.

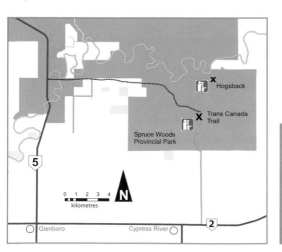

As you travel the trail, keep a sharp lookout for the Northern Prairie Skink, Manitoba's only true lizard. Skinks are extremely rare and part of a remnant population found here and nowhere else in the province. One of its strangest characteristics is the ability to "drop" its tail when tugged. When a predator tugs the tail, the skink makes a getaway leaving its wiggling tail to distract the predator.

Prickly-pear and pincushion cacti are two interesting plant species you are likely to see here. They are particularly beautiful to behold in late spring when their blossoms appear. The contrast between the harsh cactus and its delicate showy blossom is amazing.

pincushion cactus

Pembina Valley

chapter 6

Pembina River

Rossendale Area Wildlife Lands

fly agaric

Sightings

white-tailed deer
coyote
red fox
indigo bunting
red-eyed vireo

From Portage la Prairie, go 24 km west on the Trans-Canada Highway. Turn on Provincial Road 242 and go 24 km south. The site is on the west side. Go a km south to reach the Assiniboine River.

Looking northwest from the Assiniboine River Bridge, the view is magnificent. The valley walls rise to dominate the horizon, and the beautiful hues of green along the tree-lined valley offer sharp contrast against the brilliant blue sky.

The Assiniboine River winds along the broad valley bottom while the adjacent forest provides wildlife habitat. Forests remain here mostly because the valley walls are too steep and rugged for agriculture. Wildlife reaps the benefit of this cover which it uses as a travel corridor and breeding habitat.

As you gaze northwest, the land near the top of the valley is wildlife management area (WMA) with 480-acres of Crown land available for hiking and nature observation. This is one of ten small parcels of Crown land comprising the Lower Assiniboine Unit of the Whitemud Watershed WMA.

The wildlife lands located at the crest of the valley are easily accessible from the east side by entering from Highway 242. If you delve into the heart of this habitat, you will be amply rewarded for your efforts, with plenty of special nature sights and sounds. Nearer the southwest corner, the trail leads to an opening where panoramic views of the valley appear.

White-tailed deer here seem just as curious about you. The mushrooms here are plentiful and come in a wide array of colours including bright shades of yellow, orange and red.

The WMA is Crown land available for enjoyment of everyone who would like to visit

here. It is set aside for wildlife; however, this particular spot has a ski trail system. Depending on the time of year, the trails provide excellent hiking paths, although areas can be wet and not well marked.

Binney Nature Preserve

Binney Wayside is a tiny pocket of wilderness that has escaped development through the years. It is the perfect place to take a closer look at the local prairie flora and fauna. Binney was originally named after the old railway siding here in the 1880's.

Local school children and others wanting to learn about nature have visited Binney through the years, creating a demand for protection and public access. This need for nature education and interpretation led to the development of a boardwalk and viewing tower that contributes to visitors' nature experience.

A trail network takes visitors through an aspen bluff, prairie and a marsh. Blue-winged teal and gadwall ducks paddle through the reeds while blackbirds and song sparrows provide background music. Small mammals like raccoons, mink, and weasels are not always visible, but their presence is noticed in tracks and scats. Nearby the haunting hooting of owls is heard while hawks often patrol the bluffs and prairies searching for prey.

While a visit to Binney Nature Preserve is enjoyable; your adventure should not be limited to one spot. The surrounding roads are great for an evening drive past prairie sloughs, bluffs and prairie. You are in the right place, now go ahead and explore.

barn owl

Sightings

horned owl
savannah and song sparrow
hooded lady's-tresses

From Manitou, go 3.2 km north on PR 244 and 3.2 km west.

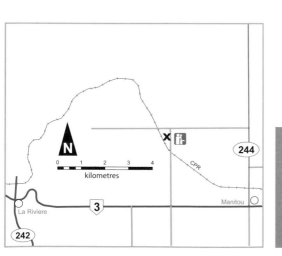

Pembina Valley Provincial Park

Breathtaking panoramic views are the trademark of this, one of Manitoba's newest provincial parks. Hikers wander through a southern hardwood forest that ranges up and down the valley walls, eventually reaching scenic vistas that are nothing short of spectacular.

The Park consists of about 440-acres of hardwood forest, mainly oak and aspen, where a creek and its tributaries cut through rolling hills. When promoting this area for park status, the Nature Conservancy of Canada described it as, "a rare natural habitat and home to over 150 species of plants and animals."

This Park represents the region's most significant landform, the Pembina Valley. The hills are part of the Pembina Escarpment, which is a section of the Manitoba Escarpment. Facilities are basic but visitors are able to explore, following a variety of trails, although some of these are quite rigorous and steep. All provide a window to the depth of the valley habitat as well as unequalled opportunities to enjoy a natural setting.

Animal signs are evident everywhere. Squirrels chatter in the trees, white-tailed deer poke from the bushes, ruffed grouse drum nearby and butterflies flit among the wildflowers, especially where the forest openings allow sunlight to penetrate. Clearly songbirds thrive, their calls heard at every pause on a calm day.

black-eyed Susan

red-tailed hawk

Sightings

native flowers
northern harrier
Cooper's and red-tailed hawk American kestrel
merlin

From Morden, go west on Highway 3 to Highway 31 and go south 21 km. Turn east on Provincial Road 201 for five km. Go south 0.5 km to the park entrance.

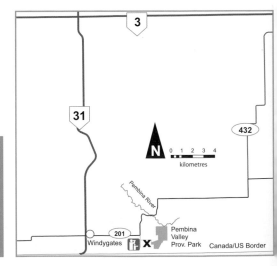

Mount Nebo

Mount Nebo isn't your typical hill. At its crest you feel that you are virtually at the top of the world with a panoramic view in all directions.

As you ascend the Pembina Escarpment on the way to Mount Nebo, you sense the height gained, but it isn't until you reach the top and gaze back that you realize how high you have climbed.

For generations, local people have made pilgrimages here, and some say this is a place of special significance that goes beyond a mere scenic view, so they hold it in reverence. Visitors usually agree.

Long known as a local landmark, this hilltop, capped with bur oak, rose, vetch, and other plant species, is one of the highest peaks on this part of the escarpment.

This is a unique and rare landform formed about 300,000 years ago and survived the most recent glacial advance some 20,000 years ago

It is what lies beneath the hill and in the adjoining region that impresses many! Eighty million-year-old mosasaur and fish fossils are found nearby in what was once a shallow sea bed. Mosasaurs are large prehistoric marine reptiles.

The area near Mt. Nebo is best known for its bentonite clay that was actively quarried here for many years and where fossils are often found. The Morden Museum currently carries on active fossil digs nearby.

When you visit do not contribute to erosion or cause any unnecessary harm. Mt. Nebo is located on private property.

Sightings
red-tailed
Swainson's hawk
wildflowers

From Morden, go 11 km north on Provincial Road 432. Turn west and go 11.6 km.

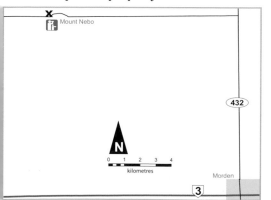

Snow Valley

red-tailed hawk

This twisting track through thickly wooded steep valley walls of Snow Valley offers exceptional views of this unusual and dramatic landscape. It is hard to imagine that anything so spectacular could be so well concealed in this thriving valley.

Deep, rugged valleys, tall trees, scenic views. Some would say this topography is out of place in Southern Manitoba. However a trip from Roseisle to Ste. Lupicin, through this region known locally as Snow Valley, will dispel any doubt!

The deeply rugged tree-lined valley here teems with wildlife. Wild turkeys, white-tailed deer, ruffed grouse drumming and the haunting cries of the coyotes will make you want to stop and listen for more sounds of the valley and its inhabitants. This is a wondrous array of nature's musicians charming visitors who join them here.

Many birds, especially songbirds, nest near the banks of rivers and creeks where food sources are plentiful and nesting cover is abundant. This combination of food and shelter contributes to a region brimming with nature spectaculars.

As in other parts of the Pembina Hills region, hawks are plentiful, and although they are far from being the only attraction, they alone would make the trip here worthwhile.

Sightings

wild turkey
red-tailed hawk and Swainson's hawk
American redstart
white-tailed deer
coyote

From Carman, go 24 km west on Provincial Road 245 to Roseisle. Head southwest out of town along the valley road to St. Lupicin.

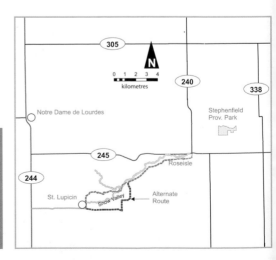

Southeast *chapter 7*

big bluestem

Agassiz Interpretive Trail

tall coneflower

yellow lady's slipper

western prairie fringed-orchid, Richard Reeves

Imagine a sea of chest-high grass waving in the wind, spreading out as far as the eye can see. Before the arrival of European settlers, much of the area south of Winnipeg was a vast expanse of Tall Grass Prairie, covering more than 1.5 million acres. Today less than half of one percent remains.

Of the remaining prairie, by 2006 a tract of nearly 23,000 acres comprised the Manitoba Tall Grass Prairie Preserve near the towns of Tolstoi and Gardenton, of which 18,000 acres have been protected by the Nature Conservancy of Canada (NCC).

This nature trail is an excellent place to experience the tall-grass prairie, view the abundance of wild plants and gain an appreciation for this important natural region. The shorter 1.6 km loop leads through aspen stands and prairie grassland where you will find one of the most prolific patches of western prairie fringed-orchid in existence. A side trail leads through a denser stand of aspen forest, then enters a large sedge meadow and leads back to the short loop for the last 800 m.

True native tall-grass prairie is distinguished from other types of habitat by the diversity of plants growing there. This prairie near Gardenton is no exception with 356 documented plant species. Along with the diversity of flora, there is an abundance of songbirds for viewing in their natural environment. More than 878 species of plants, animals and insects are known to live here.

Sightings

small white lady's slipper
western prairie fringed-orchid
lady's-tresses
sweet grass
sandhill crane

From Winnipeg, go 81 km south on Provincial Highway 59. At the junction of Provincial Road 201, turn east and go 11.5 km. The trailhead is on the north side.

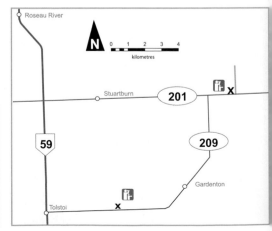

The Tall Grass Prairie Preserve is amazing. Among its most important benefits is the biological diversity that exists in these areas that have been left completely natural. With the influence of cultivation removed, this genetic reservoir remains.

Throughout this preserve you'll find a variety of endangered species including the western prairie fringed-orchid, small white lady's slipper, the threatened Dakota skipper, Culver's root and Riddell's goldenrod, to name just a few.

Among the grasses and the amazing display of prairie flowers is the awesome diversity of butterflies with 50 or more kinds present at times, including the rare Powesheik skipper. This is the only place where it is found in Canada.

One visit to the tall-grass prairie is never enough because the scene changes almost daily; so be sure to plan for another visit and be sure to bring a plant guide.

Rat River Swamp

Rat River Swamp is a vibrant wetland alive with waterfowl-viewing opportunities and easily accessed; unlike venturing into the heart of other significant wetlands. It is a designated heritage marsh.

Here you find broods of ducks drifting over the surface and, with luck, you may hear or see a least bittern along the shoreline. This is one of only two places where the least bittern was found during a recent survey.

A ring dyke constructed around its edge created the marsh cell, providing flood protection along the Rat River by impounding spring melt waters. It also created an attractive breeding and staging area for waterfowl.

This cell is part of a large system rising from its headwaters near Zhoda and in the Caliento Bog, and draining northeast, emptying into the Red River near Ste. Agathe, with many twists and turns along the way.

Where the swamp is located is actually part of the 2,600-acre Rat River Wildlife Management Area.

Surrounding the marsh cell is an upland that supports a vigorous aspen forest. The aspen forest is excellent white-tailed deer and grouse habitat.

This is an interesting location to experience nature, although it is not the only local site worth visiting. St. Malo WMA is nearby, providing a good place to watch wildlife. There are no formal trails, but the road on the north side and the cut line on the west side provide access if you have good boots and plenty of energy. A walk here will provide an opportunity to observe an aspen-oak forest setting with a reasonable expectation of seeing white-tailed deer and other animals.

great blue heron

Sightings

swamp sparrow
common yellowthroat
ring-necked duck
ruffed grouse
least bittern

From Winnipeg, go 70 km south on Highway 59. This takes you through St. Malo. Turn east and go 6.4 km to Rat River Swamp.

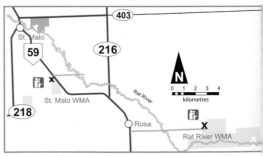

Wampum

With huge red pines towering overhead, the serenity of this mature forest is awe-inspiring and instils in visitors an overpowering respect for nature.

The red pines make one feel tiny in comparison as one stands still and quiet in the heart of the Wampum Ecological Reserve. First, you notice the silence, then a feeling of wonder creeps over you. This is no ordinary forest.

This ecological reserve is a mixed deciduous and coniferous forest with mature stands of red pine. Try reaching your arms around one of these massive trunks to appreciate their enormous size.

These straight, towering trees regenerate naturally, providing a strong gene pool for future generations, superior trees chosen by nature's selection process.

This forest abounds with other life; the signs are obvious. Perhaps you'll notice claw marks on the base of a tree, telling you that black bears, although not within view, are never far away. Listen and you may hear the chatter of an angry red squirrel, upset by this intrusion on his territory. Watch the forest floor for squirrel middens, piles of conifer cone scales, where squirrels sit to eat seeds and discard the scales. This is a sure sign red squirrels frequent the forest.

Along the trail you may notice a pile of scat from a prowling coyote eking out his existence hunting throughout the forest. Poke it apart and you'll see pieces of fur and bone from voles, shrews and other forest dwellers that fell victim to the coyote, reflecting the natural

great gray owl

Sightings

black bear
ruffed grouse
northern forest owls
boreal owl
northern saw-whet

From the junction of Highway 12 and Highway 89 at Piney, drive east for 11 km to the Wampum road and go 1.6 km south. Turn west and go 0.8 km. Turn south and go three km. Turn west and go 2.4 km then turn north and go 2.4 to the furbearer refuge boundary. Park and walk one km west.

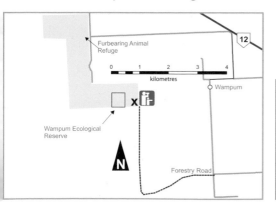

Furbearing Animal Refuge

0 1 2 3 4
kilometres

12

Wampum

Wampum Ecological Reserve

N

Forestry Road

processes that make a forest function, the never-ending "web of life".

What amazes many people is the lush ground cover: ferns, potentilla, lily-of-the-valley and other plants make up the understory. The mature canopy allows sufficient light to penetrate and sustain the understory.

While the red pine is clearly king of this forest, it is not the only attraction; the reserve is surrounded by a furbearing animal refuge.

Both the reserve and the refuge are surrounded by the much larger Sandilands Provincial Forest. As the name implies, the whole region is sandy land and rolling tree-covered terrain, a picturesque part of the province, to say the least. Exploring the forestry roads and trails provides breathtaking views and avenues to the heart of the forest. Some of these trails are best suited for four-wheel drive vehicles; however, the trails are also perfect for hiking.

Ditches, roadsides and cut-lines show that despite the forest setting, you are in a tall-grass prairie zone where big bluestem sways in the summer breeze. Flowers bloom wherever enough light penetrates. Ferns, bearberry and blueberry flourish.

While in the area, do visit the Wampum Provincial Forest, located nearby.

Sandilands

The highway sounds are muted as you wind your way south of the Trans-Canada Highway and the forest slowly engulfs you. You are in the Sandilands, one of Manitoba's oldest provincial forests — comprising nearly 3,000 sq. km — and close to the Sandilands Forest Centre.

At first, most people notice the sandy soil here and the unmistakable aroma of a pine forest. Jack pine and other forest trees thrive in this environment, but nearby is the Whitemouth River where the habitat changes as you get closer to the river.

Provincial forests were established to help protect and manage the forests of the region, and they also provide expansive tracts of public land for hiking, nature observation and other outdoor enjoyment.

Just south of the highway is the Sandilands Forest Centre. During regular operating hours, visitors are welcome to explore the centre and hike the interpretive trails. The trails explain the ecological functions of the forest and help identify many native trees and plants.

Outside its normal operating season, this is still a great place to park and explore the public roads on foot, or to hike throughout the forest.

The same road continues beyond the forest centre turnoff, providing a very interesting and scenic drive into the depths of the Sandilands. There are many trails and forestry roads that branch off, perfect for exploring. You are sure to see many forest creatures including black bear and white-tailed deer, or at least their tracks.

Sightings

American woodcock
pine warbler
spruce grouse
wild ginger
carrion flower

From Winnipeg, drive east on the Trans-Canada Highway to Hadashville. At the junction of Highway 11, turn south and go 1.6 km and turn west. Go 0.8 km to the Forest Interpretive Centre entrance.

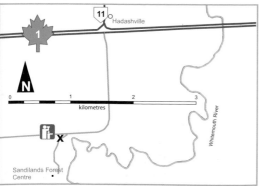

Project 13

Parks Canada

Dennis Wiens

Sightings

great gray and great horned owls
northern hawk
northern saw-whet
neo-tropical migrant songbirds
spruce grouse

From Steinbach, travel 44 km southeast on Highway 12 to Project 13, located on the north side.

Tall, elegant trees grace both sides along most of the Project 13 road. Extending between Highway 12 and Marchand, this is an excellent place to experience Manitoba's southeastern forest while indulging in exceptional white-tailed deer and owl-viewing opportunities. This is predominantly aspen forest interspersed with bog, containing spruce, tamarack and white cedar.

When you head north from Highway 12, the west side of the trail is part of the Watson P. Davidson Wildlife Management Area (WMA) which a bit farther north occurs on both sides of the road. This is a very large WMA consisting of about 14,600 acres and was the first one formed, in 1961. Project 13 is perfect as a hiking trail with owls often observed along the way. Eventually this trail leads all the way to the Trans-Canada Highway.

Long known as Project 13, this was once part of an important network of forestry roads throughout southeastern Manitoba. "Fireguard roads" allow access to the forests for fire fighting while doubling as firebreaks and a line-of-defence in the event of advancing forest fires.

According to the area's senior forester, "the reason these trails were called 'projects' is because they were cleared and built as part of the old depression work relief program, and the number was just a reference number so that workers could refer to their current job."

This trail is no longer well maintained and vehicle travel is not recommended because of frequent wash-outs, but all-terrain vehicles regularly travel here.

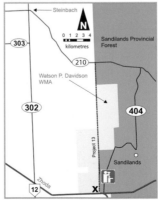

Near the north end of the trail is the Pocock Ecological Reserve about 6 km east of Marchand in Sec 27 Twp. 5 Rge. 9 E. It contains a bog lake and an uncommon species, the ironwood tree.

Whiteshell Provincial Park

Milner Ridge

Bob Jordan

Sightings

broad-winged hawk
red-tailed hawk
sharp-shinned hawk
pine grosbeak
northern goshawk

From Beausejour, travel east 16 km to Provincial Road 214. Go north on PR 214.

Milner Ridge is a natural land bridge connecting different habitats and natural regions. Many wildlife species follow this height-of-land, using it as a travel corridor. The well-drained ridge is colonized by jackpine and nearby you find moister sites with a variety of habitat and their inhabitants.

This ridge was formed by glaciers more than 8,000 years ago. It rises slightly higher than the lower topography nearby where lower, wetter sites support black spruce and other forest stands.

For some people, the Milner Ridge Road is merely a shortcut between Lac du Bonnet and Beausejour. For others, it is an opportunity to slow down and appreciate the smaller things including roadside wildlife that we often tend to overlook.

You might see a red squirrel scurry along the branch of a tree or a red-tailed hawk gliding into a treetop. Indigo buntings are known to breed in the area. Wildlife likes this ridge for good reason.

One of the best times to visit Milner Ridge is on a hot summer day. The dry heat provides a distinct feeling along the ridge's forest. Dry pine needles crackle underfoot along with the unique buzzing sound often found in forests. This shrill chorus is actually a cicada, a large insect that looks somewhat like a combinationdragonfly/cockroach.

A watchful eye should detect birds adapted to the Milner Ridge forest, such as the pine

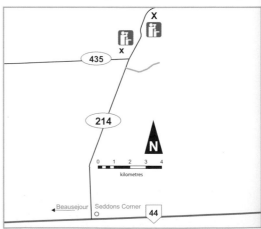

warbler. You will also find a variety of shrubs such as bunchberry, beaked hazel, an occasional blueberry, aster, snowberries, and herbs including wild sarsaparilla. White-tailed deer, snowshoe hare, vole, pine grosbeak, evening grosbeak and pine warbler could be watching you as you look for them.

You may consider swinging west on PR 435 where the first few kilometres are within Agassiz Provincial Forest. Here you will pass through a mixed-wood forest complete with a variety of wildflowers and wildlife. Watch for butterflies, which are plentiful here, and interesting birds such as the Connecticut warbler and yellow-bellied flycatcher.

false sunflower

Pinawa Road

Darlene Perkin

white admiral

Sightings

hooded merganser
black bear
red fox
great gray owl
bufflehead

From Beausejour, go east on Highway 44 for 32 km. Turn north and go 10 km. Turn east on Provincial Highway 211; the Pinawa Road.

Frequent travellers along Provincial Highway 211 take Great Gray Owl sightings for granted. They are a relatively common occurrence for those who pass here regularly.

This highway, often called the Pinawa Road, is one of the best places for observing these majestic birds. Often referred to as the "Phantom of the Northern Forest", this is one of a birdwatcher's most sought-after species. In summer these owls are reclusive with secretive habits, so are rarely seen. Winter is the best time to see them along roadsides. Perhaps because this owl was designated as "Manitoba's Provincial Bird", seeing one is a thrilling experience.

With a wingspan reaching up to 1.5 metres, great gray owls move majestically through the air and are highly regarded for their stealthy attacks when they silently swoop down to catch mice and other rodents under deep snow.

If you are lucky enough to see one of these very large nocturnal predators with its radar dish-like face and piercing yellow eyes, chances are it will be perched on a fence post or a tree limb listening for its prey.

Owls are not the only wildlife you are likely to see. The black spruce and tamarack swamp found along the road provides habitat for a variety of wildlife. As well, the "goose pond" along the road is perfect for waterfowl viewing. Birds such as white-winged crossbill, black-backed and three-toed woodpecker are also found here.

Be careful because this road has steep shoulders and it may be difficult to park. Rather than returning along the same route, try going north to Lac du Bonnet on Provincial Road 520. This is an excellent birding road.

Meditation Lake

On a still summer evening, the sun slowly sets, casting a crimson hue across Meditation Lake. A peaceful calm engulfs this setting and your mind clears, turning to simpler thoughts, leaving little doubt as to how this place earned its name. A calm, quiet evening is a great time to contemplate life from this lakeshore.

Listen and watch carefully as you silently approach the water's edge. Bald eagles are fond of perching in the tall spruce trees along the shore and the mournful cry of a loon lends itself often to the lake's tranquillity. It is a special place to visit.

This site preserves its solitude because it is not accessible by road, leaving the annoyances of traffic far behind. It is reached by a short walk along a trail.

Meditation Lake is just one of many sparkling clear lakes that combine to make the Whiteshell Provincial Park a world-class destination. Covering more than 1,000 sq. km within the Boreal Shield ecological zone, it is one of the largest parks in Manitoba's park system, and an easily accessible year-round playground, offering wildlife-viewing opportunities.

Songbirds are common here in addition to the rich diversity of waterbirds. Moose are the largest mammals here and white-tailed deer are very common. Occasionally the eerie cry of a cougar shatters the serenity. Other mammals include the snowshoe hare, lynx and red squirrel. The park provides a bountiful supply of plants and wildflowers.

Wildlife, scenery and the solitude of nature combine, making this one of the nation's best parks. The park has a checklist of bird species longer than your arm, including the Nashville warbler and chipping sparrow.

common loon, Dave McArthur

Sightings

black bear
white-tailed deer and moose
great gray owl
common loon
ruffed grouse

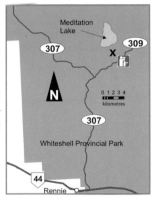

Meditation Lake

307

309

X

N

0 1 2 3 4
kilometres

307

Whiteshell Provincial Park

44

Rennie

From Rennie, go two km east on Highway 44 and turn north on PR 307. Travel 24 km north to the junction of PR 309 and go east until you reach the Meditation Lake turnoff. Go one km north to the parking area and walk to the lake.

Gull Lake

showy lady's slipper

calypso orchid, Eugene Reimer

pitcherplant

Sightings

28 species of native orchids
pitcher plant
sundew
rare and endangered species
mink
moccasin-flower

From Winnipeg, go 60 km north on Provincial Highway 59, to the junction of Provincial Road 319. Turn west and continue to Road 38E (formerly called Stoney Point Road) and go 2.1 km. The bog is on the east side and extends to Hwy 59.

Gull Lake Wetland, which includes the Brokenhead Ecological Reserve, is an oasis of tranquil beauty where rare and endangered plants abound. According to the Native Orchid Society, this wetland has a greater number of rare and unusual plants — including orchids and carnivorous plants — than any other site known in Manitoba.

Visitors should avoid the ecologically sensitive areas where rare plants grow. Instead, view from a distance or concentrate on the west side. Wherever you wander, you'll need your rubber boots to explore as this is a wet site with no markings to guide visitors.

Part of the boggy area is rimmed with old-growth eastern white cedar with characteristic flat-ridged reddish-brown bark. This cool, dark, fragrant cedar stand forms the perfect entranceway to the bog.

Eyes turn quickly to the showy lady's slipper, one of the most eye-catching plants here. But they are not the only true treasure trove. Other orchids include: small round-leaved orchid, ram's head lady's slipper, dragon's mouth, grass pink; fairy slipper, long-bracted orchid; spotted coralroot, striped coralroot, tall leafy white orchid and hooker's orchid. Carnivorous plants, including the sundew and pitcher plant, add to the diversity.

In all, this 1,391-acre ecologically significant area contains 28 species of orchids among its

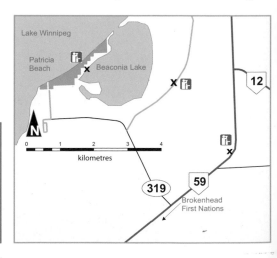

255 plant species identified so far. Twenty-four of these plant species are considered rare in Manitoba.

Recently the red damselfly was observed here, its first known occurrence in Manitoba.

Nearby you will find Patricia Beach, a beautiful sandy area that attracts summer visitors, providing unique nature-viewing opportunities in the lagoon found between a ridge of dunes along the lakeshore and the uplands. This lagoon behind the dunes, known locally as Beaconia Lake, is home to an interesting assortment of waterfowl and other wildlife. A walk along this stretch of beach will reveal a number of shorebird species that use this habitat, including an occasional piping plover.

When you visit the Gull Lake Wetland, exercise extreme caution to prevent harm to this fragile ecosystem. Visitors will appreciate plans for the construction of an interpretive trail and boardwalk to allow visitor access without harming the delicate site.

great blue heron

North Star Trail

aster

moccasin-flower, Eugene Reimer

A stand of pencil-straight pine trees tower over the southern entranceway to the North Star Trail in the Belair Provincial Forest. They are an estimated 100 years old, mere saplings when many of the region's European settlers arrived.

For nearly a century, the Belair Provincial Forest has provided a sustainable forest yield to fuel the local economy. Through the North Star Trail, you gain an appreciation for the region's history while experiencing the western edge of the Boreal Shield Forest.

This is a working forest that has experienced logging, gravel extraction and other uses.

Despite the impact of man, in this managed forest you can still enjoy nature here and see the "wild" side that the Boreal Shield Forest offers. Taking the 25-km-long North Star Trail is a great way to learn about the region and to gain appreciation for the local flora and fauna. Most of this trail system has served as logging trails so vehicles are allowed, although hiking or biking is the preferred option.

Trail brochures normally available at the trailhead help to explain trail features. For example, bird listening posts located along the south portion are good places to hear an ovenbird or chestnut-sided warbler. These are just two of the many migrant birds found here.

Sightings

gray jay and blue jay
black bear
Labrador tea
blueberry
bearberry

From Winnipeg, go 71 km north on Highway 59. Turn east on PR 304 and go seven km.

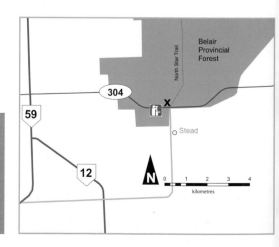

Interlake chapter 9

Hecla Island

Wavey Creek and North Mound

fringed gentian

mallard, Tammy Olson

Wave after wave of Canada and snow geese skim low over Wavey Creek before dropping into the shelter of Oak Hammock Marsh, one of the most important waterfowl staging areas in North America.

Many visitors to Oak Hammock Marsh often focus on the visitor centre and the extreme south end. To gain a true appreciation for the marsh, explore beyond the boardwalks and enjoy the depths and far corners of this wetland complex. Make no mistake: this is not a substitute for the marsh but a way to expand your experience by ensuring you enjoy all the area has to offer from end to end.

Located on the extreme north end of Oak Hammock Marsh, Wavey Creek channels water from Oak Hammock and eventually into Netley Marsh, located about 20 km northeast, and from there into Lake Winnipeg. A dyked channel between Wavey Creek and the control structure at the north mound is a good location to view native birds up close and personal.

Walking slowly along the dyked creek banks allows opportunities to see a variety of shorebirds and waterbirds. You might catch glimpses of Wilson's snipe, greater yellowlegs, or least sandpiper. Nearby you may see a marbled godwit or Wilson's phalarope. Black-crowned night heron, American bittern and great blue heron are sometimes found here as well. With a bit of luck and good timing you may also catch sight of a snowy egret or cattle egret. This is also a great place to get a close

Sightings

Wilson's snipe
black-crowned night heron
marbled godwit
Wilson's phalarope
American bittern

From Winnipeg, take Highway 7 north for 18 km to Highway 67. Turn east for eight km and north on PR 220. Go past the Conservation Centre on the main gravel road. It is 13 km from Hwy 67 to Wavey Creek. Park here or turn south to the North Observation Mound parking.

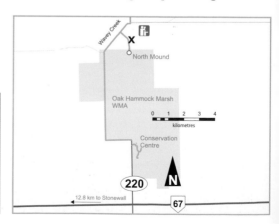

look at a variety of waterfowl including the blue-winged teal and occasionally both the green-winged and cinnamon teal.

In autumn when the marsh experiences high concentrations of geese, this is an excellent vantage point to sit and wait as large flocks return to Oak Hammock Marsh from the surrounding farm fields where they have been feeding. Sometimes they pass overhead in tens of thousands, skimming low on their final descent into the marsh.

More than 295 species of birds frequent this extensive wetland covering 36 square kilometres. Water-control dykes make excellent footpaths for a short walk or a long hike; observation mounds are found at several locations. The conservation centre is located near the south end of the marsh.

Argyle — Prime Meridian Trail

Brianna Cullen

Sightings

small white lady's slipper
coyote
red fox
wildflowers

From Stonewall, go eight km west on Highway 67. Turn north on PR 322 and go to Argyle and then go five km north on the gravel road and 0.3 km west.

Patches of magnificent native orchids growing here are only one of many reasons to explore the Prime Meridian Trail along an abandoned rail line stretching for 116 km from Fisher Branch to Grosse Isle.

A good access point to experience a snapshot of the trail is found five km north of Argyle. Here the Interlake's aspen parkland melds with the tall-grass prairie region.

Is this the point on the map where the Interlake begins? Possibly. While there is no exact point where the change occurs, visitors will pass through both these landscape types while travelling along the trail in either direction from this point. When the trail rises to cross an ancient beach ridge, you may see a patch of small white lady's slippers spreading out for several hundred yards during early summer.

Bikers and walkers who travel north find a trail lined with trembling aspen and to the south it leads through a more open farming area with patches of prairie grasses. Try going for short distances both north and south and watch along the trail for a variety of prairie flowers. However, the best patches of native prairie are near Grosse Isle.

The Interlake is renowned for its wildlife, so listen and watch for birds and animals. You may hear the cry of a coyote, so keep your ears and eyes peeled.

An interesting fact to note is the name of this trail. Our survey system divides Manitoba into section, township and range. The "prime" or Principal Meridian is an imaginary line running north and south, used by surveyors for reference in locating and describing land locations under our land survey system.

A long trail winds up and down the Interlake, opening this treasured region to visitors interested in experiencing portions of the world's most unique and critical natural habitats. Perhaps one of the best places to visit is the section of the Prime Meridian Trail between Chatfield and Narcisse, which mostly skirts the Narcisse Wildlife Management Area (WMA).

This WMA is likely best known as the world's most important red-sided garter snake denning site. More snakes concentrate here than anywhere else on earth. But the fame doesn't end there. Besides snakes, this WMA is also reputed to be world-class white-tailed deer and sharp-tailed grouse habitat.

Several "leks", or sharp-tailed grouse dancing grounds, are located nearby. At these spots the grouse return each spring to perform their courtship rituals. Along the Trail, the scenery is mainly aspen parkland frequently interspersed with open meadows, exactly the type of habitat favoured by sharp-tailed grouse.

In much of the southern Interlake one finds karst scenery. Karst is a term that describes terrain marked with funnel-shaped sinkholes found here. The sinkholes and deep cracks in the limestone allow the snakes to descend below the frost line where they hibernate.

In spring, as the sun melts away the winter's snow, red-sided garter snakes slowly emerge from their winter dens to engage in their annual mating rituals before dispersing to their summer range. The larger females

Dave McArthur

Sightings

red-sided garter snake
sharp-tailed grouse
ruffed grouse
white-tailed deer

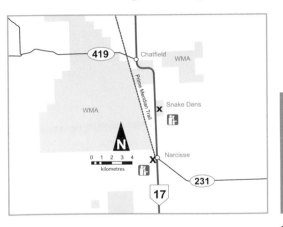

From Winnipeg, go 45 km north on Provincial Highway 7 and then 45 km northwest on Provincial Highway 17 to the community of Narcisse. Or continue six km north to the snake dens on the east side of the road.

emerge first and attract the males that become entangled with the females in large balls. Depending upon weather conditions, snakes may number in the tens of thousands as they slink and slither over the limestone, while the sound of thousands of bodies rubbing over the coarse limestone produces a loud hum. This is something which one must experience to fully appreciate.

The grasslands and meadows within this wildlife management area are Crown land and visitors can explore to view sharp-tailed grouse, and in the wooded areas, ruffed grouse.

To sample the flavour of the Prime Meridian Trail, park and bike or hike a part of the trail near Narcisse. The entire trail covers about 116 km, leading you through a variety of habitats.

Broad Valley

The high-pitched bugling sound of a bull elk in autumn sends shivers down the spine of anyone within earshot! It is unmistakable and one of nature's most powerful sounds.

Broad Valley Wildlife Management Area (WMA) is known for its elk herd as well as coyotes and other wildlife that freely roam throughout the Interlake. Elk normally bugle in September, often around the time of the first frost.

This Wildlife Management Area covers about 10,000 acres and is characterized by the lush poplar bluffs interspersed with meadows and wetlands. This type of habitat is attractive to sharp-tailed grouse, ruffed grouse, coyote, gray wolf and many other species. In winter it provides valuable habitat for white-tailed deer.

Within the wildlife management area is Otter Lake, which provides a staging area for waterfowl and other wildlife.

One of the more interesting flowering plants here is "seneca," a plant with small, white flowers and a long, woody root. The root was long considered a valuable commodity for its medicinal properties and still is.

Dennis Wiens

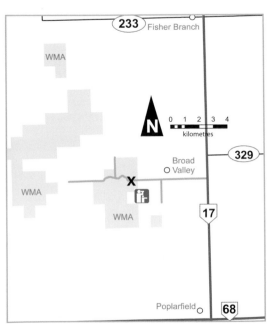

Sightings

coyote
gray wolf
sharp-tailed and ruffled grouse
red-tailed hawk
elk

From Arborg, travel 27 km west on Highway 68. Turn north on Highway 17 and go 10 km. Take the Broad Valley turnoff and travel three km. Take the gravel road on the south edge of town and go 1.6 km west to the WMA boundary.

Calder's Dock

American white pelicans glide overhead and gulls squawk as waves crash along Lake Winnipeg's rocky shore, nearly convincing one that this is the ocean. While it may look and sound like the ocean, you are actually at the next best thing, one of the largest fresh water lakes in North America. Looking east, there is nothing but open water for as far as the eye can see!

Calder's Dock is a site with a spruce-rimmed lakeshore and a cobblestone beach. Despite the scenic beauty found here, such spots are not unique along Lake Winnipeg's coastline; they are simply inaccessible. What makes this picturesque lakeshore site exceptional is the direct-road access.

While it is a long, winding drive along the lakeshore from Riverton to Calder's Dock, there is plenty of scenery along the way. After the Hecla Island turnoff, typical Interlake scenery gradually gives way to a landscape reminiscent of a northern boreal forest.

While the scenery is unequalled, there are also plants and animals for viewing, but to appreciate these you must stop and explore.

Moose, the largest member of the deer family weighing up to 600 kg, are common in the region and if you are fortunate, you could spot one locally. Moose populations are quite high, especially to the west in areas previously ravaged by forest fires. Few visitors are lucky enough to see them, but this region is also habitat for the most beautiful flower in the province, the blue flag iris, a showy plant that favours moist sites, lake edges and bogs.

If you venture along the southern shoreline, be cautious of well concealed cracks and crevices in the limestone.

Sightings

American white pelicans
black bear
common tern
gray wolf
coyote

From Riverton, go 11 km north on Highway 8 until you reach the junction of PR 234. Go 68 km north on 234 to the Calder's Dock turn off and go east to the lake.

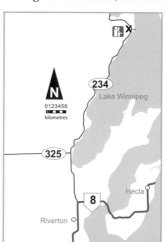

Steep Rock Cliffs

As the sun sets over Lake Manitoba, it casts brilliant crimson hues across the cliffs that rim the lake. The sparkling water, combined with changing light and the beautiful cliffs, creates scenery that is simply breathtaking!

Photographs of this scene grace many tourism publications, however it remains a place that experiences limited visits from tourists and sightseers. Those who do visit will likely agree that this is even more beautiful than any photo can portray.

This lakeshore is most unusual. The steep limestone banks rising 10-metres or more tower dramatically above the lake. In places, the waves have hollowed out the base, creating caverns that add additional beauty and mystique, ranking this place among the province's most unusual and unique places.

Trails criss-cross behind the cliffs and several lead to the base allowing views from a different perspective.

Enjoying this site should not be restricted to the cliffs, as other examples of nature's splendours await. For example, a few kilometres north lies a public beach with a great shoreline begging to be discovered. Exploring the sandy beaches or clambering over the rock-strewn shores is a delight. Shorebirds, songbirds and native plants abound.

The surrounding back roads can be explored by car. This area could be termed as representative of typical Interlake topography although most visits here are anything but typical.

Keep your eyes peeled; you could spot a coyote hunting for voles along the edge of a bluff or one of the many hawks and owls that frequent the area. Sharp-tailed grouse are also plentiful.

Sightings

belted kingfisher
gulls
American white pelican
harebells

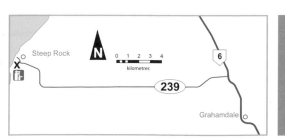

From Ashern, go north on Highway 6 for 31 km. Turn west and go 21.5 km to Steep Rock. At the public dock, turn south 0.2 km, park and go 50 metres south to the cliffs.

Lake St. George Caves

The area surrounding Lake St. George is a stunning example of Manitoba's scenic treasures that remain largely unheralded. It is also a site that demonstrates its fragility and the importance of recognizing and designating our ecological treasures.

Thousands of little brown bats hibernate in chambers lying beneath the forest floor southeast of Lake St. George. It is one of the very few places in the entire province where this is known to happen, and more bats hibernate here than in any other location. At least 13 caves are known to serve as hibernacula for little brown bats in Manitoba. The largest of these, near Lake St. George, is home to as many as 20,000 little browns each winter. These chambers are magnificent with several as large as the average home kitchen and connected by an underground corridor.

This cave and the area surrounding it are now declared as an Ecological Reserve, providing the strongest legal protection available, reflecting its ecological and geological importance. You can visit the area, but you can not enter the caves without special permission.

The caves are a feature of karst topography shaped largely by meltwaters of the last ice age. Known as "solution caverns," they were created by water seeping through the limestone, drop by drop.

Sightings

little brown bats
limestone caves
moose
black bear
bald eagle

From Fisher Branch, head north on Highway 17, then east on PR 325 and north on PR 224 to Dallas and the intersection of a gravel road known as "Jackhead Road." The ecological reserve is located about 26 km north of Dallas.

Here is the story of the cave's discovery.

An old gentleman from Jackhead, Manitoba, walked into my office late one day. He was obviously quite excited and had a story to tell. While hunting ruffed grouse near the Jackhead road, he fired a shot, "when suddenly a creature came out of a big hole in the ground and came after me," he said. "It must have been some creature that made a hole like that."

A few days later, I drove up the Jackhead Road to look for the mysterious hole and worked a grid pattern through the forest. Although not successful on the first attempt, I finally came across two spent shotgun shell cartridges. I walked farther and there it was — a huge opening in the earth! More searching revealed other openings nearby.

One of the caves was reached through a surface opening that dropped about six metres where a long cave extended laterally for more than 20 metres. Another consisted of two caves joined by a narrow tunnel just big enough for an adult to squirm through.

News of the discovery reached the Manitoba Museum, and they visited the caves, documenting the presence of bats and additional caverns. Subsequently the Speleological Society of Manitoba did further exploration in the area, discovering the largest cave, and initiating the process to have the ecological reserve established. Until now this region was simply classified as unoccupied Crown land. So a strong lobby was mounted to protect the discovery and the site was designated as a "unique/rare" site and a "Proposed Heritage Park". This provided a small degree of protection that soon paid off.

Later, I was again travelling up the Jackhead Road on a weekend and came across heavy equipment being unloaded. Being a conservation officer, I had authority to question their intentions. They were beginning work on a power transmission line from Dallas, Manitoba, to Jackhead with the caves lying directly in their path. Since they lacked the required "permits", the equipment was halted temporarily. Negotiations with the Hydro Company quickly resulted in agreement to shift the route. The caves were saved. — *Bill Stilwell, a Conservation Officer from 1973 to 1992.*

Today you can visit the caves and enjoy the splendour of this rare region, including Lake St. George and Lake St. Andrew. These are both great places for watching bald eagles and other native birds. The entire region continues to recover from massive forest fires, adding yet another dimension to the adventure of visiting this unique region.

harebell

Vince Crichton

Dave McArthur

St. Ambroise

Bernice Kippenstein, killdeer

Sightings

Foster's tern
piping plover
yellow-headed blackbird
yellow warbler
eastern and western kingbird

From Portage la Prairie, travel east for 20 km on Highway 26. Turn north on Provincial Road 430 for 22 km.

Piping plovers are among the most threatened birds in our province, and yet Lake Manitoba's shore provides one of the best remaining hopes of seeing one. The sandy lakeshore stretches in both directions from the road's end near St. Ambroise Provincial Park, providing important nesting habitat for these endangered birds.

The surrounding area is one of the richest natural regions in the province. To the east is Lake Francis Wildlife Management Area, to the northwest is Lake Manitoba; and Clandeboye Bay is to the southwest. This area is part of a large wetland complex that collectively represents Delta Marsh, a world-renowned waterfowl area.

The Sioux Pass Self-guiding Nature Trail is a remarkable feature found in the park.

Frogs are touted as harbingers of good environmental health and judging by the prolific number of northern leopard frogs here, the St. Ambroise area and the nearby WMA are doing well.

Birdwatchers really enjoy the beach ridges along Lake Manitoba's shoreline, especially during spring and fall migration.

To the east, the Lake Francis Wildlife Management Area covers nearly 16,800 acres. It comprises wetlands, beach ridge, and tall-grass prairie habitats. The beach ridge contains hackberry, a rare species of elm. Interpretive signage along PR 411 features the tall-grass prairie where Sprague's pipit and other birds are found.

Delta Marsh is one of the world's largest freshwater marshes, encompassing 50,000 acres and stretching along the southern edge of Lake Manitoba. It is designated as a heritage marsh and as a wetland of international

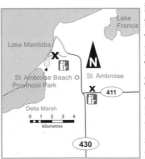

importance under the Ramsar Convention and as an Important Bird Area. The Delta Waterfowl Station, midway across the marsh, is a must see attraction complete with self-guiding interpretive trails.

Parkland chapter 10

Duck Mountain

Toutes Aides Bay

purple finch

The aquamarine water of Toutes Aides Bay looks more like a postcard from the Mediterranean than from Lake Manitoba; this is something you must see for yourself. The best place to appreciate this scenic view is at Manipogo Provincial Park.

This park is relatively small compared with others in Manitoba's park system, with few services. But it is the stunning view of the placid tree-lined bay that impresses most first-time visitors.

The park surrounds a cove, sheltered by Conrad Point jutting into the Bay, containing stretches of sandy beach frequented by shorebirds. Around the cove and further along the lake's tree-lined shoreline, migrant songbirds use this habitat as a travel corridor.

Park staff claim that Conrad Point is an "excellent bird-viewing area". Near the south end of the park, a lagoon attracts waterfowl and other wildlife.

North of the park is an interesting area with an important influence on Manitoba's history. Lake Winnipegosis and Lake Manitoba are separated by only a very narrow land bridge at this location. In the early days of the fur trade this was an important portage where travellers would cross from one lake to the other. A cairn here commemorates and explains this important part of our heritage.

Sightings

waterbirds
ruddy turnstone
neo-tropical migrant birds

From Ste. Rose du Lac, go 54 km north on Provincial Road 276. Turn right at the park entrance.

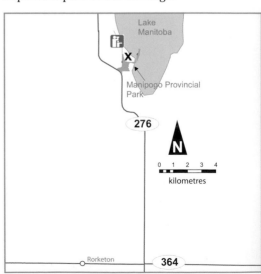

Lake Manitoba

Manipogo Provincial Park

276

N

0 1 2 3 4
kilometres

Rorketon

364

Red Deer Point

Early morning light dances over the steel blue plumage of great blue herons standing motionless, knee-deep in water along the shoreline of Red Deer Point, waiting for a hapless frog to appear or fish to swim past.

In the blink of an eye their long, pointed bill darts out to snap up breakfast. Herons are plentiful along the shoreline here as well as in the shallows along the lake-speckled point.

Local residents have known about Red Deer Point for generations but it has managed to draw little outside attention. The "Point", a limestone peninsula jutting about 50 km into Lake Winnipegosis, is revered by berry pickers, hunters, trappers and naturalists. Many wildlife species follow the shoreline and use the peninsula as a travel corridor.

You will also find plenty of ducks, geese, coots, and grebes in the coves and bays along this long, narrow, water-encircled strip of land.

In autumn, this is a special area to visit as a splash of colour streaks across the forest, turning greens to yellow and gold. The long road that twists and winds its way along the Point brings scenic views around each bend. Watch for deer, coyotes, foxes and maybe even a wolf along the way.

A remarkable shoreline is the signature feature here. Not far north along the Point, if one looks east, one sees Bachelor's Island, a place where pelicans nest.

Sightings

great blue heron
redhead
canvasback
white-tailed deer
coyote, red fox

From Dauphin, go 58 km north on Highway 20 to Winnipegosis. Continue north for 6.4 km to the Red Deer Point turnoff. Go north 23.5 km to a scenic viewpoint.

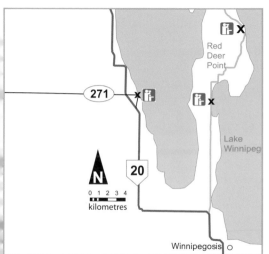

Red Deer Point

271

20

Lake Winnipeg

N
0 1 2 3 4
kilometres

Winnipegosis

Beaver Lake Road

Tall spruce, balsam fir, aspen, tamarack and other trees tower over the road as you climb the escarpment. Roadsides are littered with wildflowers of every colour and description including the beautiful fringed gentian, wood lily, giant hyssop, goldenrod, meadow rue, harebell and many others.

At first, visitors are engulfed by the solitude, but quickly realize they are not alone as ears become attuned to the forest's rhythm. The sound of the wind in the tree tops, the song of a warbler, a ruffed grouse drumming and the buzz of insects. If a journey into nature is your destination, then you have arrived.

The same exceptional scenery and habitat that make Duck Mountain a prime destination for nature lovers present themselves with slightly different faces here.

Pine River flows from its headwater atop the Manitoba escarpment in Duck Mountain and eventually drains into Lake Winnipegosis. If you head west, the road crosses a branch of the North Pine River and this is where spruce-lined banks present a great "photo op" as the water rushes down from higher elevations.

Keep your eyes peeled for wildlife as you mount each rise in the road. Moose, elk, black bear, great horned owl, hawks and other wildlife are nearby.

Farther west, the road climbs towards the escarpment's crest. Gates block the road at the Provincial Forest boundary. Continue on foot using the road as a hiking trail.

Sightings

pileated woodpecker
gray jay
dark-eyed junco
spruce grouse
lynx

From Dauphin, go 16 km west on Highway 5, turn north and go 74 km north on Highway 10 to Pine River. Go 1.6 km north and then turn west for 6.5 km on a municipal road. Note: the road is blocked by a gate at this point and is accessible only on foot.

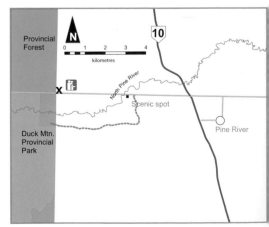

Boggy Creek

Every visit to the Boggy Creek and the Shell River area should include a climb to higher ground to experience a westward view of the surrounding countryside. For a fantastic panoramic view overlooking the Boggy Creek area, visit the Shell River Valley Nature Trail. As you gaze across this remarkable landscape, watch for elk; they are regular inhabitants.

Duck Mountain is part of the Manitoba Escarpment. After the last ice age, which ended about 10,000 years ago, this became one of the first areas to emerge as dry land.

The landscape is characterized by highlands separated by valleys created by meltwater and movement of glaciers that left an accumulation of clay, gravel and sand on the shale core. This created interesting scenery and habitat which has been colonized by a diversity of plants and animals.

Large, protected tracts of rugged land foster wildlife populations of wider-ranging species. Elk, moose, gray wolf and black bear — all benefit from this varied terrain. Occasionally cougar sightings are reported.

This region, including Duck Mountain Provincial Park, is home to a large elk herd of about 1,600 animals. In the past, herds of up to 350 elk were observed on the south and west slopes of the Ducks between the Saskatchewan border and Shell River, although numbers may fluctuate. The Shell River, both inside and outside the park, has good potential for watching wildlife.

Heading east, stop along the road and you may hear the sounds of a yappy coyote or the riveting call of a gray wolf. Nearby, Child's Lake is a popular fishing spot that offers choice bird-viewing opportunities. A favourite sound here is the plaintive call of the common loon.

Sightings

gray wolf
coyote
moose
spruce grouse
showy lady's slipper

From Roblin, go 35 km north on Highway 83. Turn east on Provincial Road 367 and go about 14 km. To reach the Shell River Valley Nature Trail, go about six km east on PR 367.

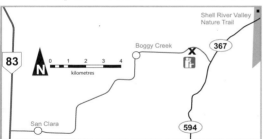

Bell Lake

Valerie Jackson

Andrea Wood

Sightings

Connecticut warbler
mourning warbler
spruce grouse
three-toed woodpecker
mink

From Swan River, go 42 km north on Highway 10. Turn west on Provincial Road 365 and go 16 km.

Rugged landscape and breathtaking views are common in the Porcupine Provincial Forest. You will find the best this region offers by venturing up the escarpment to Bell Lake. The return trip down is even more stunning, as you behold panoramic views with Swan Lake in the distance.

Porcupine Mountains ranks among the highest elevations in the province. The summit of nearby Hart Mountain is 823 metres (2,700 feet) above sea level, rivalling Baldy Mountain, Manitoba's highest point.

Bell Lake is pristine, situated at the peak of the escarpment. It is spared the influx of phosphate and other nutrient-loading faced by many other waterbodies. Instead, you have a crystal clear "gem" perched on top of the watershed.

The shoreline is not easy to walk on because it is stony and rough, although with persistence, it can be explored. You'll notice where wildfires ravaged more than two decades ago, thus starting the renewal process as a new forest grows up in the burned area. Most fires burn in fingers, leaving patches as seed-stock.

A common plant on the forest floor is bearberry or "kinnikinnick", as it is known by native people who used its leaves as a substitute for tobacco. It also has many other traditional uses.

Lucky visitors see moose and black bears from the main road, so keep careful watch.

Nearby is the Bell and Steeprock Canyons Protected Area, one of Manitoba's newest "protected spaces". Along Bell River, a backcountry trail leads hikers along rugged valleys and provides stunning scenic views; however, access is very difficult.

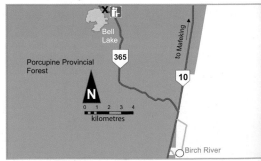

North chapter 11

Manitoba Lowlands National Park Proposal

Valerie Jackson

Sightings

American white pelican
Caspian tern
bald eagle
piping plover
lynx

From Winnipeg, go 349 km north to Grand Rapids on Highway 6. This site covers a vast, undeveloped region with Long Point located south of Grand Rapids and Sturgeon Gill Point and Little Limestone Lake to the north. They are reached off Highway 6.

Limestone Point, located north of Grand Rapids, is the longest sand spit in the entire nation. It runs for kilometres with long, sandy beaches stretching as far as the eye can see.

Nearer to the south end is another phenomenal natural feature, Long Point. Jutting nearly 40 km into Lake Winnipeg, it is an esker with sandy north shore, a rocky southern exposure and lush boreal forests in between. An esker is a long narrow ridge of sand and gravel deposited by glacial meltwaters. Shorebirds, eagles, pelicans and other wildlife await visitors to this area that is currently reserved as part of a proposed national park.

The Manitoba Lowlands is an extensive natural region covering a large portion of the province in the area around Grand Rapids. What distinguishes this particular portion is the natural beauty and scenic landforms with abundant wildlife viewing opportunities.

The proposed park includes both Long Point and Limestone Point. Long Point is magnificent. Sandy shorelines, high storm beaches and calm lagoons behind help make this the most dynamic scenery imaginable.

The Limestone Bay segment contains lengthy stretches of limestone cobble shoreline as well as scenic features of the karst landform. Sturgeon Gill Point is one of the most breathtaking features.

Nearby other unique natural features are found. One is the caves where northern long-eared bats are known to hibernate.

Another interesting feature is Little Limestone Lake, considered to be the finest example of a marl lake in the world. Marl is created when calcite, a constituent of limestone, is chemically precipitated from warm water causing the water to appear like milk with a touch of blue.

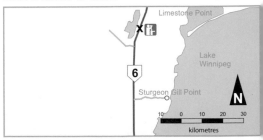

Known for its picturesque setting, this large, northern lake is dotted with tree-covered islands while its shores are rimmed with northern boreal forest. This is the Canadian north at its finest, complete with wolves, loons, lynx, and all the other wildlife you would expect to find in this Precambrian Shield environment. This is also one of the most visitor-friendly places in which to enjoy a true northern experience.

Paint Lake is the centrepiece in one of Manitoba's most impressive provincial parks with the same name. This is a place that has enjoyed visitors for hundreds of years. One early visitor was Samuel Hearne who documented a stop here back in 1774, while Native People camped here much earlier.

Coffee Cove provides a gorgeous view of the lake. Described as a "geological wonder," it formed from pillow lava, created many million years ago by ancient volcanoes.

A walk along the Cove's nature trail is perhaps the perfect way to develop an appreciation and understanding of the area's pristine beauty. It affords spectacular views of the lake and forested islands and you are likely to enjoy a bounty of songbirds.

Watch for bald eagles, as they breed nearby. Along the shore you may spot ducks such as the goldeneye or common merganser.

Many side roads offer great hiking. While there is no certainty of seeing a moose, you will undoubtedly see droppings and places where they have browsed on woody shrubs.

No visit to the area would be complete without a trip to nearby Pisew Falls. Pisew is Cree for lynx. These 13-metre high falls, which are connected to Paint Lake by the Grass River system, are truly one of Manitoba's most spectacular natural wonders.

Linda Boys

Sightings

bald eagle
gray jay
blackburnian warbler
ruffed grouse
spruce grouse

From Thompson, go 32 km south on Provincial Hwy. 6 to the park access road.

Pisew Falls: Go 73 km south of Thompson on Highway 6. Watch for the signs along the highway which lead to the parking area.

The Pas "Important Bird Area"

This site ranks high among the Important Bird Areas (IBA) of Manitoba. There is such a variety of birds here that it attracts bird watchers from great distances and people interested in wildlife viewing from around the world.

But keep your eyes open. Although the local canvasback population helped secure the IBA status, you are just as likely to hear the screech of the bald eagle overhead, see songbirds flit through the bushes or catch a glimpse of a huge bull moose. This is wild country where wildlife abounds in every direction.

Designated as an IBA under the Canadian IBA program, it is also recognized as an area of global significance based on the number of canvasbacks and other waterfowl. During a recent survey on Reader Lake, a single breeding colony of eared grebes was found to have more than 700 pairs.

The IBA contains all the wetlands surrounding The Pas, largely comprising the Saskeram and Tom Lamb Wildlife Management Areas and the Carrot River Triangle.

Saskeram is a marshy area west of The Pas, consisting of Saskatchewan River Delta and Saskeram Lake. Much of the area has been designated as a wildlife management area covering 239,785 acres of Crown land, making this one of the largest wildlife management areas in the province.

Known for muskrat production, this is an excellent place to visit marsh habitat and to view wildlife in a northern setting. Of particular interest are the nesting colonies of terns, grebes, and Franklin's gulls. Remember, there is no easy access and you see little marsh from the road.

Sightings

muskrat
black bear
eared grebe
Bonaparte's gull
bald eagle

From The Pas, go 8.6 km west on Provincial Road 283 to Turk Road. There is no specific access point so contact Manitoba Conservation in The Pas for local driving routes.

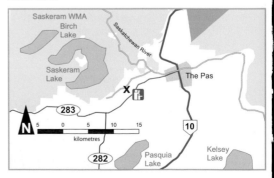

Climb the viewing tower at Bakers Narrows and enjoy a breathtaking panoramic view of Lake Athapapuskow, one of Manitoba's most beautiful lakes. This island-speckled lake's rugged shoreline is rimmed with boreal forest.

Bald eagles soar and the eerie cry of the common loon shatters the serenity of this idyllic setting. Canadian Shield lakes are best known for their crystal clear water and unspoiled wilderness. Athapap is no exception, as witnessed from the viewing tower or by taking a more in-depth journey into the region.

An accessible way to gain appreciation of the boreal shield region is by driving north on the "old" Highway 10 west of Baker's Narrows. This winding road follows the western shoreline of the lake's north arm before swinging around the top of Schist Lake. Beaver ponds and lakes provide superb scenery along the way. Grebes, mergansers, moose, black bear and other wildlife are never far off. This old highway eventually re-joins Highway 10, allowing for a circle tour without having to backtrack.

For a real taste of the Canadian Shield, consider a side trip to Grass River Provincial Park. Few places can top the majestic scenery where the howl of the gray wolf and cry of the loon greet visitors.

More than 200 years ago, this region was travelled by explorer and trader Samuel Hearne when he charted this untamed wilderness. Today it continues to attract explorers from around the world, interested in visiting wilderness and northern lakes.

This is home to many large mammals including woodland caribou, moose and wolf. The famous Grass River system — a canoe route considered to be one of the continent's best — is prominently featured here.

Glenn Smith

Sightings

bald eagle
common loon
gray wolf
wolverine
woodland caribou

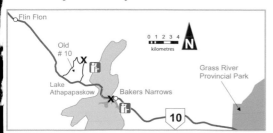

Bakers Narrows Viewing Tower: From Flin Flon, go 30 km south on Highway 10.

Grass River Corridor. From The Pas, go 74 km north on Provincial Highway 10. Turn east on Provincial Highway 39.

Index